Acclaim for Alexis Wilson

"Alexis Wilson invites us into her inner most thoughts and memories of her family with such profound eloquence, the reader is left both devastated and uplifted. Her story, exceptionally written and deeply expressed, is many things; not the least of which is a glimpse into a father/daughter relationship. As a father, it is my prayer that my daughter will one day hold me with such high esteem, as Alexis does hers. *Not So Black and White* is an inspiration!"

-Blair Underwood-
Award Winning Actor/Producer/Activist

"*Not So Black and White* is imperishably mesmerizing. Cinematically written, it effortlessly pulls you into the most intimate, heartrending of spaces between father and daughter on and off stage. From Harlem to Holland, it is a beautiful testament and tribute to unshakable love."

-Victoria Rowell-
Award Winning Actress/ NYT Bestselling author
(*The Women Who Raised Me: A Memoir* and *Secrets of a Soap Opera Diva: A Novel*) /child advocate AECF.org

"*Not So Black and White* is inspirational! Alexis Wilson is a beautiful writer. This daughter honors her father, and shares her life and love for that father, whose path I was fortunate to have crossed. Billy Wilson taught his daughter the love she now fully understands. Through her writing, she has done this with eloquence and passion. Her father is beaming that handsome smile and dancing wildly among the stars. Fly Billy!"

-Chita Rivera-
Dancer & Broadway icon

"Alexis Wilson nudges beautifully at the choices one makes and the reader comes to the conclusion that there are no "bad" choices, just choices, human choices. She makes you feel that at the end of the day, we're just human beings trying to do the best with what we've got, to be as happy as we can. Ms. Wilson is a writer whose words touch the heart and makes you re-examine your own life. Now that's great writing!"

-Maurice Hines-
Choreographer & Director

"*Not So Black and White* is a stunning memoir about an unconventional childhood. A poignant meditation on life, death, art, love, and commitment that goes to the heart of what it means to be a family. Both heartwarming and heart-wrenching, Alexis Wilson's book is ultimately a mirror in which we see our own humanity and the enduring power of love."

-Kasi Lemmons-
Writer/Filmmaker(*Eve's Bayou* /*Talk To Me*)

"A moving story of love, hope, and faith told through the journey of a devoted daughter and the relationship with her exceptional father. Altogether heartwarming and inspiring."

-Tamara Tunie-
Actress(*Law&Order SVU*) & Producer
(*Tony Award winner SPRING AWAKENING*)

"While reading Alexis Wilson's poignant and revealing reflections, on this very colorful ballet that has been her life, I found myself sitting 8th row centre on the aisle in a very beautiful theater watching a show I wished would never end. She very candidly invited me into the trunk she was born into with humor, bravery and honesty. *Not So Black and White* stayed with me long after the last page. Alexis has altered my views on life, love, loss and the discovery of who we really are. Hopefully this book is just a preview in this beautiful author's show."

-Anthony Barrile-
Actor/Screenwriter/Tony Nominated Producer

"*Not So Black and White* is the compelling and moving account of a woman who refused to be defeated by the obstacles placed before her. In her eloquent prose, Alexis Wilson writes how she learned to forgive—and even be thankful—after coming through circumstances that would have left others with resentment. This book is a story of family, of triumph, and most of all, a story about love."

-Michael B. Coleman Mayor, City of Columbus, Ohio-

Not So
Black and White

Alexis Wilson

Dedication

I DEDICATE THIS BOOK to my father, Billy Wilson, Chip Garnett, Karel Shook, Lorenzo James, Maurice Hines, Arthur Mitchell, Byron Stripling, and the rest of the cherished men in my life. You have been my heroes, my buoy, my best examples, my mentors, and my constant supporters; never expecting less than my best and never abandoning my artist's dream to succeed!

"Farther along we'll know all about it
Farther along we'll understand why.
Cheer up my brother, live in the sunshine
We'll understand it all by and by.
We'll understand it all by and by."

-from a gospel song-

Contents

CONTENTS

Foreword

ALTHOUGH I'M AN ACTOR, the element that always drives me is the story.

Every once in a while, a story comes along that touches you in such a way that you want to share it with everyone. NOT SO BLACK AND WHITE is such a story.

I have been fortunate to know the author and her father, beginning with my days at Carnegie-Mellon University in Pittsburgh, Pennsylvania, when I was studying to be an actor. Although my primary goal always has been to be an actor, I focused on honing my skills in the three disciplines of acting, dancing, and singing—and this was my mind- set when I met Billy Wilson in 1983.

From the fall of 1982 to December 1984, when I was a student at Carnegie-Mellon, Billy was head of the dance department and directed me in the main stage production of Guys and Dolls, in which I played Harry the Horse. Billy was a taskmaster because he expected and demanded only the best from his students. He was also a father and teacher of life who clearly loved his students and reveled in their accomplishments big and small.

By the winter of 1984, I was facing financial challenges, and remaining in college was becoming more and more improbable. During the Christmas holiday, I decided to tell Billy that I was planning to take a leave of absence from CMU. I asked if he would be willing to introduce me to his agent in

New York, as he had offered only a few months earlier. Although his original offer was meant to follow my graduation, he understood how pressing the matter was and how determined I was to make my move to the big city immediately. In the first week of January 1985, my mother and I drove to New York in a blizzard to secure a lead on either a waiter's job or a place to reside for the next months ... or years. Billy had invited us to his home in New Jersey to discuss a game plan for meeting his agent. The unexpected highlight of the trip was meeting Billy's daughter, Holly (aka Alexis). She was then a high school student and I was leaving college. From the moment I first met her, I recognized a bright light of wisdom and talent that was undeniable but that fact wouldn't hit me again until many years later.

I received a phone call from Holly out of the blue one day. We hadn't been in touch since her father had passed and I'd sent her a copy of a very popular book at the time about grief and grieving. We got caught up but her real reason for calling was to share that she'd written a book and would I read it? I'd read wonderful poetry that she'd written throughout the years but had no idea she'd traded in her dancing for serious writing. I replied that of course I would read it but forewarned her that aside from being embarrassed to admit that I don't read books as quickly as I'd like, I was also in the middle of a very busy time with projects I was committed to. In her typically sweet way, she assured me that she understood, to take as much time as needed, and that she was simply appreciative that I would consider the request given how busy I was.

Fast forward to several months later, much later than I'm sure she had expected, I called to announce that I had finally read her manuscript. What I wasn't expecting was the effect her written story would have on me. It wasn't just because the writing was evocative and painted a picture that immediately transported me or because of the many years of friendship with the author to know firsthand some of her ups and downs. The story is compelling and far-reaching because on a deeper level it connects with feelings of family, honesty and that funny thing we call love. I recognized that this was a bigger and more important story that needed to be told. Like theater, TV and movies, there is something in it for everyone. If you've ever been singled out for your difference, if someone you love has left you behind, if you've struggled with grief, been fascinated with an artist's life or love a celebration of triumph over challenge you will want to read this story.

Incidentally, Billy did make the call to his agent Perry Kipperman at Writer's and Artist's Agency, who was kind enough to take the meeting with me. Perry became my first agent. Soon after would follow the role on LA Law, and the rest is history. It is not an exaggeration to note that I owe the start of my career to one Billy Wilson, to whom I will forever be indebted.

In the same way that Billy had supported and encouraged me, I have tried in my own way to remind his daughter of her many gifts begging to be shared. I am proud to know her and see the woman, mother, wife, and brilliant writer she has become. She has an extraordinary life story that continues to evolve in wonderfully complex and fascinating ways. She has accomplished more than the writing of a memoir; she has opened her soul and exposed truths that most of us would hesitate to acknowledge, much less embrace. Her story—raw, painfully honest, insightful, and ultimately hopeful—is a story of a life being lived boldly, brilliantly, and without apologies.

Holly, by opening your soul, you have spread your wings! Fly high, and as these words you have penned in the following pages defy gravity and reach your father's soul, remember that the same gift of love he gave you, you've granted us by sharing your story.

We thank you.

Blair Underwood

Introduction

TODAY IS VALENTINE'S DAY, 2008. Instead of spending this charming, heartfelt holiday with my family, I'm stuck on the tarmac of Flight #1267 in Columbus, Ohio, en route to The Netherlands. As I gaze out of the window of the plane watching a hectic scene, the Oompa Loompa-like workers in their bright orange vests bustle to get us air bound.

It suddenly occurs to me that this is my Geraldine Page moment: my "Trip to Bountiful." I'm on my way to where it all began: where my parents met and fell in love dancing together; where I was born, where my brother and I visited off and on throughout our childhood; and where I fell in love and married the first time in my 20's. Now, at the age of 42, some 14 years later, I sit here prepared to travel back to my native Holland. Although this trip is business, my former husband, whom I haven't seen in 17 years, will pick me up at the Dutch airport. It is also not of small significance that my estranged mother lives in the land of windmills as well.

For some reason, whenever I fly, I feel closer to my father. I suppose there's a sense that this might be the nearest I can come to where he might now hover. And if I haven't thought about him for a while, all at once emotions surface overwhelmingly. After all the many years of his not being here, there are still monumental moments when I feel at the mercy of some sorrow and invariably unload. I do nothing to provoke the cascades of tears that come at such moments. They simply come.

Once in the air, I look out at the quiet splendor of the voluptuous clouds and feel my father in my present piece of heaven. I then ask myself why it is that at this age, after all this time of healing, I still come unglued? I berate myself for the momentary weakness, but with a bit of sudden turbulence I am brought back to my purpose of this journey. I remind myself that the object of my trip is to redeem the integrity of my father's work, stolen by producers who used it without asking me first.

However, as I sit here at 30,000 feet, a seat away from a young woman who is coughing and hacking and clearly not feeling her best, I realize I have absolutely no idea what to expect. I wonder, will I be triumphant or will I skulk back with my tail between my legs, having fucked the whole thing up because I wasn't really up to task? Which will it be? I have to decide. For weeks preceding this trip I gave off an air of unshakable conviction and moxie at pursuing the producers in an effort to do the right thing. But here, in the belly of this vessel, I am privately struggling with much. It all comes bubbling up. Without question, the decade or more that has passed has left me a more complete, fuller woman than I ever thought possible. Yet I still question my strength.

As the wash of blue now coalesces into a palette of reds, oranges, and yellows in a sunset sky far above my smaller worlds, I am given grace to float away and think about much. I slide into reverie, remembering the cast of characters who have played the important roles in my life: my mother, my father, my brother, Chip, Chi-Chi, and a select few others. They visit me with laughter and sadness as I try to put all the pieces together in my head.

In what way have all these souls rubbed off in making me who I am at this moment? I decide then and there, with an almost suffocating desperation, to figure it out before I land where I was born. The burning sky beckons an inner excavation, a rewind, and I travel back in time in my mind. As usual the comforting voice of my father comes to mind:

"I shall always be foolish but I shall be alive until the end. I want to leave my children a legacy of life. They will know that they sprang from the loins of a living and vital man. Not free from mistakes but free enough to make mistakes. Lusty and alive. No apologies, only a guideline constructed from the best stuff I've got—me."

(Taken from my father's diary
December 10, 1972: Boston)

For the first time, I saw my world in such tremendous terms. A blaring, blinding white light flooded over me. The planet was suddenly so large. I can recall the day, soon after he died in 1994, when the permanence of my father's absence hit me in the stomach so profoundly and acutely that I thought I might float away.

I was running around doing errands on that bright and sunny day, along with men in their comfy faded moss green tees, mothers in walking shorts shuttling their newborns and contrary three-year-olds into the Giant Eagle grocery store. It dawned on me, clobbered me, that my father was not coming back. He was really gone. Not only was he gone—gone from his house, from his work, from picking up the telephone, from New York and New Jersey, from this country and Europe—but he was also nowhere else on Earth. Nowhere on this entire planet would I run into him. No longer could I summon his wisdom, feel the security and comfort of his always-right words and count on the reassurance that everything would be okay. He had always been here, sometimes miles, oceans, states and countries away—but always here.

God, how I loved him, admired him, was frustrated with him, and inspired by him. That familiar pain in my heart revisits me yet again. I hope it never ends. Loss is painful, but I never want to lose the impact of his memory upon me. On that sunny day, doing my errands and trying to go about my normal activities, life caught up. It does that. It snatches you unaware and says, "Did you think I forgot about that? *You* haven't forgotten about it, have you?" It does it sometimes at the most difficult and lonely times ... grinning. On that day it grabbed me by the jugular and shook me around. I was flailing for an explanation and a little mercy. Then grief slowly let me down and loosened its grip. I heard my father's voice, as I often still do, saying "This too shall pass, Holly. It will get better. Keep moving forward; there's work to be done. You have a great and exciting journey ahead of you. It's just part of the process, darling. Life happens to everyone. And don't be discouraged when you don't find all the answers. Look for answers in the grey. Life's not so black and white."

Rememberings nudge me further and more deeply. I'm suddenly struck by the need and uncomfortable urge to travel in my mind to where all of our stories begin. I adored my father but my mother is the one who brought me into this world.

Chapter 1

SONJA

I HAVE SEEN MY MOTHER three times in some thirty years. Still, despite nearly all the mother/daughter memories lost, I have retained a clear picture of her as if she were standing here before me right now. She wears a lavender turban of a thin gauzy material or a black furry hat, depending on the weather. She hates the cold, as I do. She is chic, but just this side of kitsch. No earrings, although her ears are pierced—unless by now they've closed. Her make-up is light in quantity but clearly professional. A hint of color to the cheeks. Brows penciled in and defined. Her eyes are unremarkable brown eyes, but no doubt my father saw their unique beauty. She sweeps a liquid liner on the lids in a theatrical yet subtle way. Less is more. Her eyes are done in the fashion of the '50s when elegant women wore suits of black bouclé and the fashion template was Dovima. There is a lateral greediness to my mother's lips, emphasized in a pinkish salmon or red hue, then filled in with the same. If caught in a thankless light, the slightest hint of blonde facial hair can be detected just above the lips and on her white cheeks.

Ash blonde is her original hair color. She always dyed it auburn for the stage. Wisps would often escape from beneath her hat or wrap. A slightly pointed nose. More than anything I recall an inoffensive mole on the back of her neck. I remember her beauty marks.

My mother was not a striking beauty. Not in the face. Her face was—and is—pretty, but her beauty, her sex appeal, is in her carriage—the unmistakable grace of a great dancer; how she glides from this place to that; how her small head is delicately balanced atop her swan-like neck when she responds to you. It is in the way she crosses her legs and also in the lyrical adagio of her effortless gestures. Since the last time I saw her she remains, in my mind, graceful and lovely in this way—always standing out in a room and parting a way where there was no way before she walked in.

I imagine her still wearing a tightly fitted black or magenta stretch turtleneck with Lycra-like black pants. It is a style stuck in the '80s, mixed with classic European taste—her ensemble made complete with black or grey suede high-heeled boots that armor up the length of her long slender legs. This is Sonja Maria Magdalena van Beers, my mother, on the outside. What I've felt about her on the inside is a much more varied and complicated story.

She was what they used to call a "baby ballerina." These were the supremely gifted girls who, from the time they could plié, were on stage dancing full-length ballets as stars. Her legs, feet, and line were exquisite. She could linger endlessly in a balance on pointe and had mastered the beautiful art of bourée as if floating across a stage, her feet fluttering like a hummingbird's wings. My father said that he'd never seen a more beautiful Sylphide than the one danced by my mother.

These very young dancers, while being hailed as classical phenoms, also were protected, pampered, and made fully dependent upon the ballet for everything. In some instances, though not all, they were hopelessly spoiled and emotionally underdeveloped. In my mother's case, it seems that this pampering might have contributed to who she later became and partially explain some of the regrettable choices she made.

She had been the golden child of Directress Madame Sonia Gaskell's National Ballet of Holland (later named the Dutch National Ballet) and endlessly indulged. When the opportunity arose to dance the technically demanding roles, like that of the Black Swan in Swan Lake, she was allowed to bow out and opt instead for the adagio and more lyrical roles. At the time, holding all the cards might have made her feel privileged and in control. However, in the long run, she developed an uncanny knack for sudden injury when she was scheduled to dance challenging roles.

My late godfather, Karel Shook, who was the ballet master of the Dutch company in the '50s, foretold that Madame Gaskell's spoiling would prove disastrous for my mother's career and cripple her character for years to come. It seemed that much of his prediction did come true, though not until years later.

Her growing years remain a mystery to me. Regardless of what her childhood may have been during the war years—and I'm sure, like most of the Dutch population, she had her share of sadness, disappointment, hardship, and deprivation—dancing made her happy. And it was dancing that would introduce her to my father, Billy Wilson.

Billy had been dancing in the European company of *West Side Story*, starring Chita Rivera, in London, when someone from the Dutch ballet who had seen him in the show approached him about joining The National Ballet of Holland. Excited by a new opportunity and one that he'd dreamed of as a kid, he accepted and made the trip to Holland.

My mother was seventeen when my father was invited to join the company as a guest soloist. He was twenty-one and already married to a pretty Philadelphia girl from a well-to-do black family. He caused quite an "exotic" and intriguing sensation as one, if not the, premier black danseur performing with a celebrated European classical ballet company at that time. The internationally renowned choreographer Serge Lifar was so impressed with my father in his ballet *Suite en Blanc* that he created a special ballet for him: *Othello*. My mother danced the role of Desdemona. Lifar's *Othello* was the role and the ballet to catapult my father into international ballet stardom. The year was 1958. My mother and father were both oozing with the electricity of talent, youth, beauty, and tremendous sex appeal. They were stars on the horizon of the European ballet world and soon would fall madly in love.

Billy had married his first wife at nineteen, knowing he was too young and not ready. He soon became aware of how different their interests were and was already impatient with his wife's penchant for boredom. As sparks began flickering between him and my mother, he made a call home with a last plea for his wife to join him. She declined. When he returned to the fresh-faced Sonja, who looked up at him with wonder and the sweet smile of promise, he knew one chapter was ending as a new one was beginning. With all of their obvious commonalties and not-so-obvious differences, their love affair was wonderful in the beginning—as many beginnings are.

It didn't matter that he was a bit older, already married, and African American. They were mad for one another. My parents were drinking in their romance and soaking up their success. He was puffing out all of the machismo and ego that came with newfound ballet stardom. His brown rippling muscles were no doubt sending her swooning, as her milky white skin and high insteps were making him dizzy. The recipe for thrill and excitement was undeniable. Everywhere they went, in each city they performed—from Stockholm to Madrid—they were treated like royalty and often lunched with them.

They danced the great ballets together in a blitz of celebration and European adoration. They were sensational together. On and off stage they created frenzy. In Italy, children ran up to my father and touched his skin to see if his color would rub off. However, in Europe he felt that the children's actions were the result of a genuine curiosity, as opposed to a freakish curse or condemnation. The conversation in Europe was not about how the ballet could allow this interracial arrangement to exist but what would be the next debut piece they would perform together. Meanwhile, back in the States, the Black Revolution was exploding. Different times, different attitudes, different countries.

On March 8, 1965, they were married, and in October of that year I was born in The Hague. Weeks before my birth, my father returned to the United States to begin teaching and heading the dance department at Brandeis University. The civilized and celebrated life he had been living in Europe during the previous decade could no longer justify his remaining there while African Americans were in the midst of important change. He did not want to experience these times by proxy.

The States

Their reunion happened soon after I was born. When I was two weeks old, my mother brought me to New England by plane. We lived in a snow-covered house in the middle of a deep wood in Waltham, Massachusetts, while my father worked at Brandeis.

My young dancing mother had a lot on her plate: learning a new language as she left behind the protective and familiar world of the ballet. It was a brave and inspiring journey.

Whatever she did not do as a mother later, I look back on the time surrounding my birth with admiration and pride for her display of physical and mental courage. If only that strength had continued and were linked to a necklace of loving examples I could remember! Perhaps then the pattern of seeping dysfunction would end, and my daughters today would have a grandmother to know, to touch, and to cherish. If only there were no "if onlys."

Instead, there are giant gaps, black holes, and spaces when I try to recall fond memories of the time spent with my mother. It is an inexplicable desert of not remembering. Even my therapist, many years later, found it odd that I wasn't and still am unable to access positive places in memories attached to my mother. Historically, this kind of shutdown is triggered by a traumatic event—a rape, physical or verbal abuse—something. In my case, that didn't happen; there's simply nothing there.

My father was astonished to discover my lack of memory of happy times with my mother. He would fondly reminisce and share some amusing story I couldn't recall. "Oh, come on, Holly," he'd say, Holly being his nickname for my middle name—Holliday. "You must remember that. We were happy in the beginning. It's amazing to me that you don't remember the happier times when we were all together." The lack of remembering made me feel ashamed. What I do remember in detail are difficult time, angry times, and snatches of solitary moments with my mother.

We moved to Boston in 1969. During the early years, my parents worked hard and created much. They founded their own dance school and company—The Dance Theater of Boston—that toured the Netherlands Antilles in the Caribbean. We spent our days in rehearsal rooms and running on white beaches. Those were inspired and productive years for my parents. After a few years of struggling, they dissolved the company and my father became one of the creators of the children's television show ZOOM, doing all the staging and musical numbers. He won an Emmy for the show, and he loved every moment of working on that project.

In Boston, I remember climbing on jungle gyms, getting dirty, and wearing my favorite smock. It had tiny flowers sewn all over it and two pockets outlined in bright yellow. Do children even wear smocks anymore? I remember playing with pastels and crayons, loving any form of drawing or painting. I remember playing with clay and mixing it with water. The cool ooze would run through my fingers and the softness would cake hard under my nails. That's what I remember. But not much about my mother.

Parker

After Brandeis and a series of moves, we landed in a red brick brownstone on West Brookline Street, my favorite home in Boston. We spent some important time growing up on that lovely, tree-lined block full of children and parents who all knew one another.

Around the corner was a small and sedate version of Spanish Harlem. It was a very mixed-up neighborhood, which is why we fit in perfectly. There were hot summers on West Brookline Street—long evenings when adults would sit out on the stoop until dark. My father would stand with one foot on a step above the other, one leg bent, the other straight, while all the children played. He'd have one hand on his hip and a chilled glass of something strong that would clink, clink with ice while he carried on quiet conversation.

While I remember my father during that period, most of my memories are of my brother, Parker, who was born in 1970.

When my parents were on holiday in Venice, Italy, before I was born, my father looked up to see the name of a street called Flavio. He liked the name so much he brought it back with him to the States and it later became my brother's middle name: Parker Flavio Wilson.

Parker had the face of an angel—a Botticelli cherub with lightly brown-sugared skin, instead of peaches 'n' cream. He had a full head of flowing ash blonde curls that I could effortlessly redirect with my fingertips. My God, he was a beautiful child, like one of the startling Brazilian children from the film *Pixote*. Unfortunately, along with the beauty, a bit of sadness accompanied him upon his arrival. As a very young boy, he stopped urinating. He held it in, as if holding his sweet breath in order to make his small presence known. That attention he so desperately craved was our mother's. It seems that she was not fully prepared to have a second baby. She was perhaps more ready to think primarily about getting her life back and the time she felt she'd lost since becoming a mother.

My parents took Parker to the doctor to get help with his upsetting and potentially dangerous health situation. The doctor recommended that they take their baby boy back home and be with him, hold him, kiss him, take baths together with him, and to basically love the shit (or, in this case, the pee) out of him. They did as he suggested, and Parker began to let go and release.

That period of Parker's life always pulled terribly at my father's heart. He believed that event to be a point of departure, indicative of difficult things to come for my younger brother. He also believed the first five years of a child's life set the stage for his or her ability to cope and thrive later. His belief in that theory might have proven true in our case. My first five years were different from Parker's. My father once gingerly shared with me that he believed I had gotten the happier years of our parents' marriage. I received much doting and attention from both of them. By the time Parker was born, things had begun to disintegrate.

As a child, Parker was bright, curious, devilish, and naughty. He loved taking his clothes off and running around naked; shaking his butt and little-boy penis, especially because it embarrassed me. I remember that as a young boy he had crazy crushes on women. Always very pretty women, but grown women, not little girls. In hindsight, I view this as yet another indication that he was in search of our "absent" mother.

Parker was a natural-born dancer and exceptional at any sport he tried. He would come in from playing hard all day or riding bikes in the summer sun and glow a deep cinnamon, his young skin tawny and tight. Being five years apart in age, we did a lot of normal fighting as brother and sister, and I so resented his always needing to tag along and have him constantly under my wing. Sometimes I would hide from him, finding secret places in the house, or retreat into my room.

Our bedrooms in that house were big, like the mouths of caves, with large windows and wide planked-wood floors. They were on the third floor, second from the top. My father had his study—with its big skylight—on the top floor. I think that room was his escape. He loved it up there. The sun streaking in would create a magical mood, keeping the room aglow in unusual spots. My bedroom looked down onto the tree-lined street, while Parker's sat off the backyard facing the tall pussy willow trees that led out to our mysterious alleyway.

I played with imaginary friends, and Parker had a trunk load of dolls, from Black Raggedy Andy to G.I. Joe. We spent hours sliding down our polished wooden banister, riding bikes, or roller skating if we could find our skate keys, which often weren't around our necks. We played hopscotch and jump rope. On our front steps, we hatched our plots of hide and seek, traded Wacky Packs, and used mirrors borrowed from our mother's vanity drawer to burn the sun's rays into pieces of wood we found in trash cans.

While we played carelessly and happily outdoors, indoors our parents' ideal marriage and family were tearing bit by bit at the seams.

Hot pants

One thing I do remember about my mother in the summers of my Boston childhood was her hot pants. They were too hot, worn with heels very high and strappy. It was a display too suggestive, too obvious, and very deliberate. Something sad and screaming for attention, attention, attention!

I recall images of my mother's naked body. Both my parents, being dancers and free from much self-consciousness, displayed a confident ease with nudity and made it feel normal. Throughout our house hung several pencil drawings of them in the nude done by a Dutch artist friend. I always liked those drawings.

In my mother's dressing room hung Pucci, suede skirts, corked wedgies, and silver earrings that dangled with baubles and mirrors. It was the '70s, after all, and my parents were giving great *Mod Squad*. Everything was mini this, blouson that. Even their bedroom walls were a mod zigzag pattern of black, white, and shiny silver. But for all the heat that had once existed between them, their bedroom always felt cold. In that lovely brownstone, their marriage was freezing up and zigzagging into a jagged crack that eventually would split everything in half: their marriage, the house, and us.

My parent's differences, which in the beginning were so attractive to one another, had begun pulling them further and further a part—far enough apart, in fact, to land my father in Manhattan, where he accepted an offer to choreograph his first Broadway show, with others soon to follow. For a subsequent show during that same period, he auditioned a young and beautiful singer/dancer who would change his life forever. The young man's name was Chip Garnett. He stepped out onto the stage with his watery eyes and enormous hands, opened his mouth to let his gorgeous voice be heard, and my father knew he was special. In fact, he invited him all the way to Boston to have dinner at our home on West Brookline Street.

Chapter 2

SOMETHING BREWING

I REMEMBER THE FIRST TIME I met Chip Garnett. The scene was dark or dimly lit, in shadow. All I saw was a tall visitor with red-brown skin and enormous hands. Big bright eyes. We were in the kitchen, always one of my favorite rooms. In that usually sun-filled harmonious kitchen, discord had already begun. The house had begun making its descent into a home out of sync some years before Chip's arrival. That evening, did our mother have the slightest inkling of something romantic brewing? Knowing my mother's almost psychic intuition, as well as the general sensitivity that accompanies most women in such scenarios, I'm sure she did know *something*.

At that first encounter, Parker ran happily into Chip's endlessly long, hopeful arms. I, however, stood in the doorway, unmoving and reticent, with arms folded in front of me. I was nine years old. I wonder what we ate that evening. Was it comfort food or something more difficult to digest—something that ended up getting stuck in everyone's throats? And was this, then, *bringing him home to meet the family?* I look back now with a sour taste in my mouth at my father's bold choice. I give him the benefit of the doubt that at that time it was still a friendship and nothing more. However, I do question my father's innocence. I suspect he knew what he was doing in the same way I believe that my mother knew who she had married, which included my father's roaming eye for both women and men alike.

9

That night might have been the moment that my suspicious and distrusting nature was born. I was, without a doubt, on guard to anything that might have threatened our already fractured family life. I'm glad I don't remember any negative vibrations other than my own.

My recollection is a series of stills set against a surreal backdrop. I remember my father standing to the side, while my mother moved around the kitchen in distracted ways. It was a strange scene as I recall it; the memory of its being a bad dream, though I don't remember anything bad happening. In the air settled a suspended foreshadowing of something unwanted to come. I don't believe I got any closer to Chip as the evening wore on. Where Chip was concerned, my mistrustful and unyielding nature lasted well into my college years. It ebbed and flowed as I got older, but we always trod a bit lightly around one another. Bit by bit, over the years, we whittled our relationship down to a place where love and respect could flow freely between us, but it took a long time. It seemed I stood forever at an endless hallway of black and white tile with Chip at the other end.

Meanwhile, in the mid '70s, tension between Billy and Sonja grew. I sat one night with Parker on our staircase. Our fingers clutched at the wood spindles of our banister with our faces pushed in between them. It was past our bedtime and our parents were arguing hotly. My mother scratched the side of my father's face with her fingernails and he replied with a slap across hers. I recall nothing like that incident before or since. It was after this that my father began moving out. I was mad at my mother for "making Daddy leave."

The picture of our family had fallen and smashed into a million razor-sharp shards that flew in many confusing directions. Something had seriously altered what had been our happy family home. To this day I don't know if it was my father's betrayal with "Robyn Red-Nails" (a woman), "Sam" (a man) or Chip who ultimately caused the other shoe to drop, but something happened and it changed everything.

No one really knows what happens between two people in a marriage or a relationship but those two people. The nuances and intimacies are too complicated and too human. I am reasonably certain that along with my father's extra-marital affairs, there also existed my mother's growing frustration at having given up so much to become a mother. She manifested those feelings by excluding Parker and me more and more. I also believe that my father was the true love of my mother's life and that her particular love for him grew to obsession. Perhaps the seed had been planted before my father entered her life, gestating for someone like him to obsess about. He thought so.

Although he was crazy about her and loved her incredibly, he would tell me of her unrelenting persistence and inexhaustible determination to get what she wanted by being manipulative. There were times, before marriage and children, when he told her he would be "away" in an effort to have some time alone, and she would call. Some twenty or so rings later, exasperated, he would pick up the phone. She would then say, "I knew you were there." Her doggedness unsettled him. As time went on, she would become more manic in tone. To this day it remains recognizable in her personality. There is a certain something slightly off center, taut, on the verge of some shaky place that revealed itself more and more as time went on. Their separation got that ugly ball rolling as exchanges between my parents got nasty.

There were back-and-forth upsetting phone calls with put-downs by our mother and attempts to turn us against our father. Negative scenarios were becoming a steady part of every day, as our mother in particular began to unravel.

She made a comment to me while we were on the phone when I was ten. My brother and I were visiting Dad and Chip in New York, as they were living together by that time. With venom in her voice she exclaimed, "... your Daddy being with that *man*!" I asked what she meant by that. I didn't understand. She replied, "You know what I mean. You'll see. You'll see." She should have added, *"my pretty*!" She sounded exactly like the Wicked Witch of the West. I wasn't crazy about the idea of Chip, either, but I wasn't burdened with the vile weight of her implication. Not yet anyway.

With our father living in Manhattan, while my brother and I remained in Boston, it was a vulnerable and angry time for all of us. Living with my mother began to feel like living with an agitated and preoccupied distant friend of the family. Her responses were curt and final. This was also the time that she began to spin contrivances and tell untruths. One such story sticks out in my mind.

My mother had been teaching class at the Boston Ballet. One afternoon she was taking a class instead of teaching. A combination with jumps in the center of class led to an unfortunate accident. She and another dancer collided in the air and my mother was injured. She tore cartilage and pulled some of the ligaments around her knee. She ended up wearing a cast on that knee for a time. For an article written about her, after the cast had come off, she told a different story of how things went. She recounted that the incident had left her in a wheelchair with a cast from her neck to her toes. I read the article years later and was struck by how the karma of such dramatics surely would come back to haunt her. Perhaps it haunted me more.

Despite my child's dream of the perfect family with all four of us intact, my mother, Parker, and I moved from our home to an apartment complex. The address was 6 Whittier Place, along the Charles River. There was a gigantic sign, seen from the highway, parallel to the Charles, which read: *If You Lived Here, You'd Be Home Now.* It was neither the life nor the home I wanted to be living in.

Parker and I missed the space and warm, cozy comfort of our old brick brownstone. We missed our neighborhood friends; we missed making forts and playing hide and seek in the alleyways. No longer playing as a whole street of kids until the sun went down or hearing echoes of our parent's voices calling us in—the appetizer to our warm meals together. Living only with our mother, our family dismantled, we now ate in silence our dinners of tuna melts and Tang.

Being children, we adapted to the many changes as best we could and found new things to explore and keep us busy. The apartment was actually a part of a luxury complex. It was like a self-contained city. Everything we needed was right there; a grocery store, cleaners, and a movie theater along with indoor/outdoor swimming pools. In the summer daylight, we spent all day in the pool, diving over and over again from the high dive, trying to perfect our entrance by protecting our heads from hitting the surface too hard. At night we swam underwater, like sea creatures, down to the pool lights that created a silent magic until our lips turned purple-blue and our fingertips wrinkled like ashen raisins. The pools and the theater especially made up for some of the sadness we were feeling. It could have been a lot worse, but in our hearts the joy was seeping out.

I hated that apartment. I remember coming off the elevator to our floor. The walls and carpet were a horrible blue. Not a French blue or a Dutch blue or even an American-flag blue. It was a milky flat blue sometimes found among discarded frosted glasses and unremarkable chinaware. A reject blue. A blue that one *settles* for when one is unable to find or afford a more pleasant one. And how had we arrived at this place to live? Who decided that? Did she, did he or did they come to that decision together? Had she lost a reason to care for much more than was absolutely necessary? But that doesn't sound like my mother. Closer to what was more her way of thinking was to find something economically smart in order to pocket the rest.

I overheard a conversation she had with my father that I never forgot. We would visit him once a month if not more. My father was financially responsible for everything—including my mother's cut flowers for the apartment—except for a one-way plane ticket for us to New York. We were ready to make the trip, but my mother refused to pay the way. If he wanted to see us, he would have to pony up. He acquiesced and we got there, but the moment was upsetting. I understood enough at ten years old to know that she was creating a very ugly situation—for money.

School day

One morning while I was getting ready for school, I walked into my mother's bedroom to look at the clock, which sat on her bedside table. As I entered, I discovered a glistening, dark male body with a clean-shaven head, intertwined with my very white naked mother. In that moment, she became "white" to me for the first time. For the first time, I noticed the contrast because my mother was embracing a man other than my father. And now I saw that she was a different color. Some kind of childlike colorblind spell had been broken. I'd seen her "kiss the frog," and my view of things was altered.

I'm sure that a great many baffling thoughts swirled through my head as I stood frozen for what seemed like a very long time. It was, in fact, only an instant. An instant of computing that my mother no longer loved my father, that she was holding onto a man who was a different color than she, and that this was a secret thing I wasn't supposed to know about. I hated her for making me feel all those things I didn't fully understand. I know that I ran out of that room like my heart was on fire—out of that room, down the cold noisy stairwell, and out of that damned blue building.

In hindsight, I look back upon that unsettling event and wonder what my mother must have felt. For all I know, that may have been one of the first sweet moments in reclaiming some of her lost power, in regaining some of her self-worth, her femininity, her ability to attract, and her sense of once again feeling desirable. It was probably all of those things. For sure, it was my mother's private moment, not meant for my young and vulnerable eyes. An array of new feelings and judgments was born for me as a result of what I discovered that day, and it took some time to swish away the bitter taste left in my mouth by what I'd witnessed. After that incident, I didn't like to come home much.

By this time my mother was endlessly exasperated at not being able to keep a rein on five-year-old Parker. He had tantrums, sometimes knocking his head against the wall. What were his days like, often alone with our mother, who was distracted and numb with anger?

If I could transcend time, I would go back to 6 Whittier Place—hemmed in and trapped by the ugly blue walls and carpet—and not think only of myself. I would hold little Parker tighter, reassure him more, play with him more often, let him sleep in my bed when he needed that extra comfort, and make sure he felt wanted and protected when things got rocky. We all needed something, but I wasn't getting it at home with my mother.

"Take them"

It became clear to my father that some new arrangement had to be made. My mother's destructive behavior, crafty manipulations, and neglect of us were growing. My report cards from Chestnut Hill School were sent from my mother to my father unopened. Other correspondences revealed conversations between my father and my teachers, who clearly were concerned about my mother's lack of interest and involvement with me and my schooling.

By that time, Parker and I were flying back and forth to New York to visit our father and Chip more frequently. Our mother would send us there with a suitcase filled with dirty clothes meant for Chip to wash and with pants that hit above our ankles because she wasn't spending the money for us on us. Upon our arrival, our father would be fuming and close to tears at the same time. Something had to give.

At the other end of a bloody battle, change was coming. It was 1976 and the divorce was in full swing. Just when things had gotten as upsetting as possible, my mother shocked everyone even more, including her own attorney, when, in a real *Kramer vs. Kramer* moment, she said to my father, "Take them." This was the only reason my father, a black man in the early '70s in Boston, Massachusetts, was able to obtain full custody of both his young children. We were six and eleven when we came to live with our father and Chip.

Chapter 3

NEW YORK, NEW YORK!

WE WERE A little scared and a lot confused. We desperately wanted a life that was *back to normal.* We were not only being shuttled from Boston to New York, on a monthly or bi-monthly basis, but we were also being shuttled from mother to father ... and Chip. After a relatively short time, following my father's having won custody, we moved permanently to live with them to 375 Riverside Drive on 110th Street in the city—Manhattan. I loved that apartment. It sat on the rounded corner of the drive and a stone's throw away from the Hudson River. The building is still a lovely old brick, with elegant wooden doors and brass hardware. They used to shine the brass. I relished, with a private excitement, the fact that the doorknobs gleamed. It was like entering Oz. The old wood paneling smelled of coffee grounds and lemon peel.

We were at home in that apartment with the same comfort and simple elegance we had been accustomed to in our red brick brownstone in Boston. Even the kitchen wallpaper, made to look like Mediterranean tiles of a white, cobalt, and olive green design, was nearly identical to what we had on our old kitchen walls. A small and humble country French table sat against one of the walls. The space was small, like a *peek* of a kitchen. Right off the kitchen was a maid's room. Next to that sat the dining room. It was a comfortable expanse, filled by a mahogany table and six matching high-backed chairs upholstered in a Missoni-inspired design. Each chair cover zigzagged with muted tones of salmon, brown, soft greens, and crimson. In the corner of that room there stood a pale-yellow silk Chinese screen framed in black lacquered wood, with a bird scene depicted on its three panels. It was a lovely screen that later lost its life due to an irreparable tear through the silk of its most elaborate bird. The room looked out through big windows onto the Hudson River. In the summer we'd open the windows in the evening and beckon a more tranquil side of Manhattan to join our table for light dinner fare.

I recall that the apartment felt more like a house, and though it ran on a single level, it seemed to go on forever. The living room was the hang. My father and Chip would put on Earth, Wind & Fire and we'd dance for hours to "September" and "That's The Way of the World." In that space sat an endless cinnamon-brown brushed cotton ottoman that snaked around most of the room. The ottoman had ten to twelve pieces to it, and beneath it lay an off-white shag rug. It was the comfort zone of the apartment and for my brother a cushiony jungle gym. Parker was forever jumping all over it. Dark shiny wood floors led us from room to room. Around the corner to the right sat Dad's bedroom of cherry and bamboo furniture. Terracotta walls, browns, oranges, and brick reds all came together in paisley bedding. The windows were draped in brown moiré. The accents in the room were brass, and the outline of the door panels and crown molding had been painstakingly painted with a tiny sable brush dipped in gold leaf by my father. He kept the small bottle of gold in one of his desk drawers and relished having to take it out for a needed touch up. His room was masculine and elegant. And although everything was just so, it remained inviting. His bed was fluffed with a billowy down comforter and an array of expensive, sumptuous throw pillows. It was definitely where the master of the house slept and conducted business. Two phones—one black, the other cream—sat on his desk, ringing constantly into early evening. Across from my father's room was Chip's—a stark contrast to Billy's. Their tastes were often as beautifully different as they were oftentimes eerily the same. Over the years, it seemed their differences melted like warm chocolate into a common comfortable river that remained more similar. It was a thing that helped to keep them bound together for as long as they lived.

Chip's room was like walking into a solarium. It was white, bright, and bathed in sunshine. Even on wet dark days, the room held its effect of feeling turned on like a light bulb. He had come across what had become a popular bedding print called Strawberry Patch. The bed sheets were of a stark white background and all over it danced the viney curls of green tendrils that held perfectly red ripe strawberries. It was simple and fresh. Chip bought a slew of flat sheets and fastened them expertly onto every inch of wall space, including making floor-length curtains for his large windows. It was as if you'd made your way down the rabbit hole and landed amid a bright, sunny garden of summer-red berries. Upon first entering, you were struck and even overwhelmed, but once you settled, you didn't want to leave. I wanted my room to be like that. And who knew a strawberry patch gone wild could work in a man's room? But it did. It fit him, and he was comfortably at home in that fantasy of old-fashioned sweetness.

Chip and my father had created a lovely place together, complete with ample comfort, beautiful things surrounding them, and with their distinctively individual styles intact. When I took in Chip's room, with all its sweetness and charm, I thought that perhaps there might be hope for us—that we might just discover a common ground we could accept and live with. This would take longer than we both thought it would. In the meantime, my father was trying to survive my mother's wrath, but regardless to what swirled around us, we always had each other.

We three

In the mid '70s, *The New York Times* did an article on my father highlighting his successful Broadway accomplishments. They took photos of the three of us. This was during one of our visits before custody became final. The only piece of furniture Chip and my father had in the living room of their apartment was a giant ladder. That's where the *Times* wanted to take the shots. One of the pictures chosen was a stunning black-and-white eight-by-ten photo taken of my father, Parker, and me sitting on that ladder in the empty room. It is a portrait full of fierce love.

My father had two hit shows—*Bubbling Brown Sugar* and *Guys and Dolls*—running on Broadway at the same time, Tony nominations, a steady flow of royalties, new offers coming in, a partner to share it all with, as well as his children almost permanently by his side. However, with all of the success of the moment, the irony sits behind my father's eyes in that black-and-white photo.

He was in the heat of the divorce that threatened nearly all of his hard-earned bank account and the strength of his spirit. He was often nearly paralyzed in the mornings trying to brush his teeth—bent over the sink unable to straighten from the stress that sank its claws into his lower back. He got through on a steady diet of Valium chased with gin and tonics, along with Chip's tireless support. In the photo he is visibly the center of our universe, as he sits flanked by the two of us on either side, but I believe it was he who was adrift in a stormy sea and we his salvation. His eyes reveal a painful subplot, but we are all there, rock-solid in our love for one another. The other undercurrent was that while my father's battle with my mother came to a head, the one that I had with Chip was just beginning.

Despite what would clearly be a long road to acceptance in embracing Chip, being with Dad was exciting. Being in Manhattan was exciting. Parker and I took rides in the now-extinct big yellow Checker cabs with the jump seats. We fought over those black vinyl-covered jump seats that stuck to our thighs like mad in July. We were as thrilled as we were terrified to be gazing out in awe at the speedy hysteria. It was great fun and an adventure simply getting from place to place. The sights and sounds were intoxicating and made us dizzy with wonder. We were living in The Emerald City. Our father's life, work, effusive attention to us, and his *wanting* us there with him made us feel safe and special. Everything about living with our father was so much better. Except for Chip.

CHAPTER 4

THE OTHER WOMAN

MY FATHER INTRODUCED Chip to us and to everyone else as his friend. The four of us would all be going somewhere, when I would be struck by Chip's constant presence. I found myself wondering why he was still there. With my head cocked slightly, I ran the questions through my mind: *Why is he here? Who is he to my father? Why is he living with us?* What was it that I saw in those eyes as he looked into my father's? There was something there, but I didn't know what it was. In those beautiful, watery, almond-shaped eyes, there was a love that I resented and wasn't getting from my mother. Where he was letting it flow and letting it run all over us freely and unconditionally, I kept my love locked up inside for no one to share except my father. I didn't want Chip's love.

I wanted him to leave—and leave my brother and me alone. Yet he was always there, waiting, it seemed, in every corner, in every spot of the apartment, on every street corner ready to bring us home. But he wasn't *home* to me for most of my growing-up years. He was a thing I wanted removed, surgically taken away, permanently left to find his way to some other home, befriending some other man, to share some other life. It was in the eyes. In that bottomless pool of acceptance and adoration for us, there was his need for inclusion and being wholly embraced. But I threw stones into those pools and disrupted his hopes. I attempted to dash his dreams and send him packing. I was angry and I *wanted* to be angry. I didn't feel worthy to receive unconditional love from anyone other than my father. I didn't trust anyone else.

Chip and my father were friends, true, but I had friends and I didn't live with them. It had already been confusing to understand what had happened to our original family. I was just eleven and needed answers, but I didn't ask.

We now had the security of our father's steady love. Yet our new family arrangement was without question *not* the perfect tradeoff. Not only was being gay still very much in the closet, but two African American men raising two young children was even more "strange." Many things confused me. When I wasn't sleeping at night, I would hear rattling. The floorboards creaked underfoot as my father visited Chip's bedroom. The sounds made me suspicious and curious. I could hear their muffled voices. Sometimes it sounded like conversation, at other times like abrupt eruptions. There was the hint of something secret amiss—a language I didn't fully comprehend. I tried hard to listen, but the moments were hushed and the walls were not thin. I knew it was their adult time, but I was also trying to make sense of men with men.

Same-sex couples were always a part of our experience growing up. They were our closest friends, dancing partners, teachers, and lawyers. It was an arrangement we recognized and embraced as children. But new questions arose since it had become our family. I struggled with my imagination about those mysterious sounds. Did I have an ear on their intimacies? During my tweens and teens, I couldn't get a full picture of what such intimacies might look like, and that allowed my very vivid imaginings to explode. I didn't feel that it was bad; I just didn't fully understand what went on in physical terms.

My feelings attached to anything sexual were of engaging in something very wrong; the memory of my mother's compromised position and something forbidden; the obvious explanation for two men needing to hide their physical love for one another. Apart from the show of a warm embrace or a kiss on the cheek, Chip and my father never displayed anything of an intimate nature in our presence. They professed their love for one another and they were clearly a couple—in it together to make our family work—but where were the movie star kiss and passionate embrace? I felt instinctively that there were pieces of our puzzle that were missing.

My father would have said (and did upon occasion) something different. He would have said something along the lines of, "It is what it is and not everyone's going to like it." He would say that easily, but in all honesty, the climate still forced him to introduce Chip not as his lover or partner, but as his friend. The truth about my father and Chip's relationship remained secret to all those except their closest friends and the theater community. My father especially still needed to navigate in the business arena, and keeping things simple implied no need for everyone to be privy to his or their lives. They didn't completely hide it, but they also didn't flaunt it.

No doubt it would have added some deserved sweetness to their private lives if they hadn't been forced to continue their great love as only a friendship. It was, after all, bigger than that. If they'd felt they could live more freely, then the romantic Chip could have basked in public endearments and more careless displays of affection. He would have loved that. He deserved that. When you're in love, you want the whole world to know. Of course, they knew the truth about their huge relationship, but wouldn't it have fantastic had they the possibility to be completely honest with their lives?

Ah, to live in a *normal* world. However, feelings of normalcy and harmony were not yet on the menu where Chip and I were concerned. As a result, before the calm, along with all the beauty and laughter that prevailed, came a storm that raged and stayed a long time between the two of us.

Chip provided much of the stability and consistency in our home. Because of this, he ended up being the "bad cop" and the disciplinarian when my father was away. My father was incredibly disciplined and clear when it came to the rules and respect of the house and one another, but not in the same way that Chip could often be. He could be like a drill sergeant at times: meticulous. He liked his i's dotted and his t's crossed. Chip also had much more to prove in the house, needing to make up for not being our mother and not being related to us by blood. Blood or not, he still loved his new family, his career, and the fine life that he and my father were creating together. He enjoyed being taken care of to a certain extent as well. For the most part, it worked for both of them.

Though Chip had clearly paid some heavy dues during his childhood, he still had not yet paid the same kind of dues my father had weathered in regard to "the business," which gave him clout and respect in return. I believe Chip very much envied the respect and those stripes that my father had earned. He wanted that recognition, the same fees, the same kind of billing my father received and could demand. He was gradually growing tired of performing in the shadow of my father's greater success or of being offered the lesser roles. He wanted the family, a house in the suburbs, as well to be the headliner, the main event, *the star.*

As a young girl, I wasn't aware or concerned about Chip's insecurities. I only saw devices used like a wedge that I felt threatened the closeness between my father and me. Chip and I competed with one another, and as much as he got under my skin, I started to get under his. I decided, however, that I would not be daunted, defeated, or undone by his presence. No doubt, he had similar thoughts about me. Aside from his determination to be accepted by us and fulfill his dream of having a real family, he very naturally gravitated towards the role of "mother," which couldn't have rubbed me in a worse way. I was at the ready for any opportunity that displayed any attempt to tell me what to do or in any way suggest that he was a permanent replacement for my mother, although I never mentioned my mother after the divorce. In fact, I never talked to anyone, not even my nearest and dearest girlfriends, about my family life. No one ever brought up the subject. It was a topic off limits, and that included any talk about Chip.

I worked very hard at keeping my home life at home. And although the fallout from the feuding between Chip and me affected every aspect of all of our lives, the conversation never left our front door. As I grew older, I discovered it was "the Wilson way" of dealing with tough challenges. You maintained your cool, kept your sardonic and sarcastic wit about you, presented a poker face, and pressed on.

When I was a teenager, my friends knew that I couldn't stand Chip. At the same time, I was completely baffled because my friends all loved him. A few of them even had crushes on him and swooned when they were in his presence. Their acceptance of him further foiled my plan. They weren't supposed to like him. I was trying to get him gone! In the meantime, everyone respected the rules of the game, never bringing up the subject of our unconventional family arrangement. They all seemed more than agreeable to accept Chip as our "uncle" who lived with us. He had made perhaps the more palatable leap from friend to uncle.

I would tell him, "You're not my mother!" The sentiment is familiar. We've all heard it, though usually reserved for the female lead. Yet, in a sense, he was. He had, without question, assumed the more traditional female role. He did most of the cooking, he washed our clothes, organized our birthday parties, snooped through our things, and told our father everything. This behavior was normal family stuff, but I didn't like him doing any of it in the same way I'm sure I would have felt about another woman doing it. I insulted him, ignored him, and could even make him cry. He seemed the representation of all that was wrong in my world and consequently got all the shit as it hit the proverbial fan. I had made Chip's departure from our otherwise happy home my objective—and my father sat lodged right in the middle of it.

Neither Chip nor I wanted to relinquish the ground that connected us to "Billy" or "Daddy." It was like fighting for the same man. Our dynamic was not too unlike that found in Eugene O'Neill's *Mourning Becomes Electra*, which, ironically, happens to be one of my favorite plays. The only switch among the cast of characters was that my opponent was not my mother, but Chip.

However, upon deeper scrutiny, it *was* actually my mother I was fighting with. In Chip, I had met my match. We could both be manipulative and complicated. He was not easily undone. It was a stressful and often destructive trial between us and constantly tested the integrity, as well as the peace, of our family life. My father had just about reached the end of his rope and demanded that something change. He brought me into his bedroom one afternoon to tell me he wasn't "liking" me. He did not like the young lady I'd become and was disappointed because he knew I was better than that. First and foremost, I was devastated by the possibility that I could be such a disappointment to my father. I never wanted to fail him. It was for the first time that I was also struck by my own selfishness and immaturity. Some little piece of me shifted that day. Through my tears I *heard* what he said and knew I needed to let go of my anger and hurt.

In hindsight, I realize that I just needed someone to talk to—and probably someone other than my father. He tried to coax things—feelings—out of me, but I was afraid. Of what, I don't know. There was always something floating *out there* that kept me from uttering things out loud and in the open. I felt instinctively that to do so would not be a good thing and decided instead that none of those feelings would ever be shared. I would keep them to myself at all costs. I could throw them up and into the safety of my diaries and my cryptic self-indulgent poetry. I would be strong and disciplined. I would not cry but instead hold on to my feelings and confusions with a vengeance. I would stuff them as deeply into my throat as possible and I would be fine.

Chip, on the other hand, would become my emotional punching bag and receptacle for everything I kept locked up inside and everything that was wrong in my adolescent life. Both my brother and I searched for a thing to throw our angry and confused energy into: a thing all our own. Parker found it in the streets. I found it in dancing.

CHAPTER 5

AFFAIR WITH DANCE

AM TOLD THAT I was doing arabesque before I learned to walk. That may not be entirely true, but dancing was around me from my beginning. When I was only a newborn, my parents put me in a basket and took me with them while they taught their ballet classes. They set me down in front of the mirrors and began their workday. I can remember taking ballet classes taught by my parents; I was also frequently escorted out of those same classes because I tended to cause a bit of commotion, fool around, and see how far I could push the little perks of nepotism. I enjoyed the fact that my parents were dancers. It was something I was proud of. Having been born of dancing stock, I was, in my own reserved way, a ham. I loved to pose and craved much "look at me!" attention. But my serious feelings about dancing didn't come into play until I was eleven years old.

I remember my ballet clothes. I can smell the clean newness of the pink tights that felt so soft and delicious. They reminded me of stretched freshly unwrapped Bazooka bubble gum. They were sugary sweet and precious to me. I got so excited coaxing them gently out of the plastic that kept them protected and unwinding them gingerly from the cardboard around which they were perfectly folded.

The smell of little girls' salmon pink ballet slippers immediately transports me to the various magical studios I traveled through as a child and later as a young adult. Those tiny pink slippers were a Cinderella dream to many little girls enchanted with the possibility of becoming a ballerina. That possibility was also quickly getting deeper under my skin.

Once I was old enough to use a needle and thread, I sewed the elastics and ribbons onto my slippers and my point shoes. My shoes were becoming an extension of my young dancing personality. They were getting worked in and supple. Only when I wore out the toes enough to make holes in my slippers and bind them with duct tape did I feel worthy of a brand new pair, strong with the fragrance of stiff leather and suede.

My mother taught me how to wash out my dance clothes, and it became a kind of sacred and endearing ritual.

From those early days of special memories attached to dancing, the one memory that stands out, aside from the "high" of simply being on stage, was how I felt entering a very special space—The New York School of Ballet. It used to stand on 83rd Street and Broadway, and it was where I began taking class when I was eleven years old. The school and company—the U.S. Terpsichore—were led by Richard Thomas Sr. and his wife, Barbara Fallis. It was a haven for ballet dancers of every ilk, from first-timers to battle-scarred veterans.

You came upon the largest of the studios immediately upon entering the building. As you walked down a short hall from the elevator on the left, the big studio sat across from the sign-in desk. The door to that studio always remained open and when I stood in the doorway, I felt as if I were on a precipice gazing down onto some great and holy ground. A steep flight of stairs took you down to the floor. The floors were all a light wood—a thing rarely found in today's world of linoleum and veneers. The ballet barre stretched nearly all the way around the expanse of the room, with the exception of the one wall of floor-to-ceiling mirrors. The left wall was all big windows.

In winter, the smell of worn wood, traces from multitudes of overheated bodies, and the sharp scent of rosin hung suspended in the air when the room was empty, as if waiting to descend upon the hosts of willing and hungry dancers who dared to step into that room to begin the ritual all over again. In the spring, those same familiar smells seemed to waft lazily throughout the studio like sweet perfume that danced on the back of a light breeze.

The atmosphere during changes in seasons creates different experiences in a dance space. Taking classes constantly bundled, layered, and laden with so many articles of "rags" during the winter months feels very different from the total freedom of dancing nearly naked with the cooperating looseness of one's more willing limbs in the warmer months. Whatever the season, the studios and the classes offered a wealth of experiences for me to soak in.

Richard Thomas' class, often overcrowded and very alive, was full of activity, conversation, joking, and laughter. It was by no means the traditional solemn and sanctified ballet class. His classes were like a social gathering. Those who attended his lessons were devoted followers and a diverse community of loving sheep. These were dancers who embraced his biting, quick wit and tough-love approach to teaching the craft. He looked like a craggy old man who'd just rolled out of bed and into his well-worn ballet slippers. His peppered short hair was always mussed, and he would riffle through it with his hand as he thought through a combination. Although he appeared all hillbilly on the surface, with his often-crass shouting and twangy accent, the gorgeously supple and highly arched insteps of his seasoned feet gave him away. He was a kind of sheep in wolf's clothing: a grumbly cynical New Yorker with a big bite but a heart as enormous as a whale.

His wife, Barbara Fallis, who was his partner in their school, was equally endearing in a completely different way. She wore a powder-blue leotard and matching short chiffon ballet skirt; her short brown-gray hair was softly curled, framing her face like adoring clouds. Her manner was quiet and wise. Her carriage was light, and she had an ethereal twinkle in her eyes. Although they were opposites in many ways, they both possessed the thing that so many dancers migrated to their classes in want of: technique.

Technique was what The New York School of Ballet was all about, especially if you asked Richard Thomas. He would tell you so. In fact, that family had natural technique in bucketfuls. Ms. Fallis could demonstrate the entire barre—exercises for warm-up at the ballet barre before doing combinations in the center of the floor—without ever touching her wooden stool for support. She would turn to the other side without once holding on. One simply marveled at her perfect equilibrium. Their daughter, Bronwyn, was no different. Occasionally, their son, Richard Thomas Jr., who later became well known as John Boy on *The Waltons*, would visit his dancing family and take class as well. He was always lovely and very down to earth.

Technique, technique, technique. Richard, Sr. often would harp on dancers who got caught up in "too much dancing." "I don't teach dancing," he'd say. "You wanna dance, go somewhere else!" His teaching of technique was widely known and a New York institution among dancers. Between Richard Thomas and Barbara Fallis, there was something to be learned. Their style of teaching was as different from one another as their personalities.

Richard Thomas was a dyed-in-the-wool dancer. He loved dancers and teaching. And for all his brashness, he was also charming, very funny, and genuinely interested in both Parker and me. Excited by talent, he treated the two of us like an extension of his big ballet family. He encouraged us, pushed me, embarrassed me, and always pulled me front and center out into the open. He never let me hide. He was always on dancers to "get the step"; to learn the combination and reverse it. He was big on reversing everything—and making it faster.

One time, after he pulled me by the arm up to the front of the classroom, I messed up an allegro combination. He singled me out and yelled, "A dumb dancer's a dime a dozen. Holly, get the step!" I was crushed. It took me years to fully understand the larger meaning of what he was telling me. All I heard was that I was dumb.

The words from that day still ring clearly in my ears, but now I'm glad that those words and his voice continue to visit me. He would get on Chip, who was devoted to the 10:30 a.m. class, about something real or imagined, and they would continue an affectionate tête à tête throughout the remainder of the lesson. My father would often stand in the doorway before class ended, and Richard would invariably make a tongue-in-cheek announcement that the 'famous Broadway choreographer' had arrived. The comments were to be expected and accepted with grace, for below the surface was a mutual respect and sincere fondness. Richard Thomas was important to my father because of his real interest in both Parker and me. He was important to me because he ignited a fire from my already small burning ember.

Richard Thomas was instrumental in giving me my technical "base" and in shaping my growing desire to become a serious dancer. He put Parker and me on full scholarship. He and my father made an arrangement that I take no fewer than three classes a day during the summer months and that I occasionally help at the front desk. One of my required classes was the 10:30 morning class—the one Chip loved. That class made me so nervous, I would get short of breath and start to hyperventilate. Chip would always catch my eye and remind me to breathe. Even tiny Parker, at six years old, took that class, and he kept up better than I did. He breathed through the entire lesson.

In that class would be an A-list of famous dancers: Cynthia Gregory, Christine Sarry, Sean Lavery (aka Owen), Ivan Nagy, Gelsey Kirkland, Ronald Perry, and others. You never knew who you'd find stretching next to you at the barre. Although it was a professional class, dancers from all walks of life and levels came through that door at the top of the steps and all were equally welcome. It was also a ball! Pure entertainment. Richard would take the first five to ten minutes gossiping, his arms flailing; he would be followed by his faithful dog, Honey—a big red Chow—who would sit in front of the mirrors and slobber during the lessons.

Richard's hearty American twang carried all the way to the threshold, down the hall to greet you as you stepped off the elevator. If you still heard him gossiping, you knew you had time to slip in before class began. If, however, you had the grave misfortune of trying to creep in late during the barre, his bellowing would erupt from the pit of that studio, and you would be at his mercy for the rest of the class. He would then use you as fodder for the next morning's gossip.

It was a wonderful place to feel alive, full of dancers' sweat, inspirations who stood next to you at the barre, laughter, and serious work led by two unique individuals who created space for those who dared to dance. Those beautiful studios no longer exist, but the feelings, the smells, and the memories will never leave those of us who experienced the world of dance at that time. It was there that I became driven to study seriously.

At the end of my day of ballet classes, I would intentionally take my time as I sat in the girls' dressing room on one of the long, dark wooden benches. Waiting until I was nearly alone, I would self-consciously begin to change into my street clothes. Many times I would simply put my clothes on top of my leotard and tights. I did it because I was incredibly modest about my body. I was often the youngest in many professional situations, and this fact heightened my self-consciousness about my not-yet-developed body. I felt underdeveloped, but really I was just young and, like many dancers, a "late bloomer," as my father used to say. He'd tell me I came from a family of late bloomers, and that always made me feel a lot better. Later, in my teens, when I did bloom, I would be self-conscious in another way because I was often the only dancer with such an ample bosom. Be careful what you wish for!

Muscat d'Alsace

We called our godfather Chi-Chi. When I was little, I couldn't pronounce Karel and so I came up with Chi-Chi. Karel Shook was instrumental in helping to mold and shape my father into who he later became as an artist. When I think of Karel, I see him standing near the edge of the subway platform, not too unlike many New Yorkers, waiting for the express A or D train to pick him up and carry him to 145th Street and Convent Avenue. It was his daily travel to his home away from home, The Dance Theatre of Harlem— DTH, where he taught.

I see him wearing his baggy Levi's that hung, plumber-style off his hips years before it had become a calculated part of our hip-hop culture. I don't recall what he wore for a shirt. Probably a sweatshirt but he forever wore his jean jacket; a jacket I eventually conned him into giving me. It was authentically worn and torn. I wore it until it was nothing but threads.

His most memorable article was not clothing but an old, ugly shit-brown—no other color description suffices—pleather shoulder bag. He was never without it. It had a long strap that hung past his waist. It had a zipper closure, which was never used and the bag itself was never retired. My God, that bag! And that shock of full and beautifully silver-white hair against alabaster skin and always, of course, a cigarette.

They called the jazz trumpeter Conti Condoli "The Silver Fox," but Karel was my original silver fox. He was older than my father by ten or fifteen years. He stood around 5'10" and was unassuming until he got into the studio. He had petite feet, so small it seemed possible to stand him in your hands. During the ballet class, he wore soft black jazz shoes that were tightly laced.

He gave hard classes that were often excruciatingly slow, made to build your endurance and steel your stamina. He taught the lesson with a thin wooden stick to demonstrate the rhythm of it; as he tapped the floor from count to count with the piano, he meant business. I often liked to take the men's jumping class because it challenged me, but those classes were more than a notion. Karel was a taskmaster.

He was many things to my father. He was his teacher, mentor, and most cherished friend. I don't know the intimacies of what went on between them, but I'm pretty certain that early on they also had been lovers. My mother had been my father's great love, an Asian doe-eyed beauty had been a great love,

Chip had been a great love, and so had Karel. I don't even know how they first met, but I do know the all-important impact Karel had on my father as total artist. In New York and later in Europe in the mid- to late '50s, my father was a sponge soaking up all the wisdom, lessons, and knowledge that Karel selflessly shared with him.

As a mentor, he exposed the young Billy Wilson to a wealth of art, music, dance, food, and creative people. As my father told me, "Karel would say, 'This is what you need to know. Here, read this book, look at that painting, listen to this piece of music, this is the wine that goes so beautifully with this meal, and this is why." I believe he found in my father a most willing and passionate pupil and cherished friend.

As a younger man, Karel had danced with the Ballet Russe de Monte Carlo; later he opened his own school—Studio Dance Arts—in New York, and in 1959, he became ballet master of the Dutch National Ballet. He stayed in the Netherlands with the National Ballet for nine years. He was an intellectual with an often-scathing wit and a published author. He had a command of several languages, a passion for opera, was a wonderful painter, and had the gift of mastery in the kitchen.

His friends and frequent company might include opera diva Leonytne Price or ballet royalty Dame Margo Fonteyn. I had the good fortune to be introduced to both great ladies by him at one point. He knew anyone there was to know, particularly in the ballet world. Karel was this great, rich treasure that my brother and I often had all to ourselves.

When my father first joined the ballet in Holland, he lived with Karel. They would work hard in the studio, and then come back to the flat; Karel would massage my father's feet to help keep them supple, and my father would rest while Karel went to work in the kitchen. They would both unwind with an early-evening cocktail and cigarettes languorously pulled on and dramatically exhaled. It was the prelude to hours upon hours of humorous and stimulating conversation. This was the scene in the early '60s, before marriage and children. It seemed an idyllic life, and I believe that for the most part, it was. It was my father's cultivating time—a time of tough work, hard play, hard drink, and exploring with abandon. It was the art of so many things: the art of dance, culture, travel, friendships, love, and not least of all, cooking.

My godfather woke up in the morning with the day's menu on his mind. He didn't just make lists in his mind or on paper of what he hoped to achieve.

It was a routine that was accomplished. It is the way that those who are in love with cooking go about their day. For him, food was a centerpiece around which all the other loves, such as dance and friends, harmoniously revolved.

It all really concerned dinner, which might happen during lunchtime if the day was free. He garnered great satisfaction from making others feel delighted and content through his extraordinary meals. A ham and cheese sandwich would never be just a ham and cheese sandwich. It would be toasted French bread with triple-cream Brie and honey-smoked ham with sliced Jersey red tomatoes from his garden, fresh basil leaves, red onion, and a hot, nutty mustard. He always maintained the simple quality of a slightly European lifestyle as he shopped for fresh ingredients daily.

I miss that Euro-social environment he created. It was in his home when you walked into the old apartment on 8th Street in the Village in Manhattan or through the unlocked doors of his house years later on Slocum Avenue in Englewood, New Jersey. One could easily have felt as if he or she had been transported to a European flat or arrived on the breeze that whispered through the open windows of a house in the south of France. His house had that unmistakable feel and smell of sweetness and charm; however, it also was very disorganized and not terribly clean. Books were everywhere in piles on chairs and on floors, with cat hair floating amid the comfortable bohemian chaos. Upon entering that house, an adagio danced throughout the rooms with the slightest hint of Vidalia onion, homemade chicken broth with Muscat d'Alsace or Château Gilette simmering just below the surface, a waft of a mushroom roux heavy with cream and the dry fresh yeast of a baked baguette. All of these ingredients mingled with rosemary, thyme, and cigarettes.

To be in that house was intoxicating. Even without a tumbler of vodka on the rocks with a twist of lime, or a gin and tonic, one still felt woozy from the aromas and the richness of his character. He would labor tirelessly for hours over a steaming pot of some stew with chunks of the best cuts of beef that melted in your mouth like Burgundy-drenched butter. And for hours, if we were there on a weekend, we would fixate on cigarette after cigarette, as it hung lazily out of his mouth or between his long fingers. The ash at its tip would bend as long as wilting asparagus, and we watched to see if it would finally disappear into the pot. It never did.

Chip absorbed all he could from Karel's mastery of food, and no doubt it inspired him to try new and more ambitious creations. Chip cooked very much the way he baked—always precise and striving for perfect presentation. Karel's cooking was highly labor-intensive, yet seemingly improvisational because he made it look effortless. There might have been gravy stains splattered on the tablecloth or on the platter presenting the braised chicken breasts, wound with twine and tarragon, placed slightly lopsided on the Delft blue platter, but the forkful was divine! My father cooked somewhere in between, leaning closer in his style to Karel's because he rarely measured anything and loved to throw together whatever he could find.

Karel created feasts on a whole other plane. And the more he drank, as the day or evening wore on, the better the meal would be. He would finish the breads, cheeses, appetizers and entrées, plate everything, and then sit down with us. He would have a drink in one hand, cross one leg over the other with varying degrees of difficulty or ease, depending, and take a long drag off his cigarette. He would watch us all feast and talk and talk and laugh and talk. He had a very dry, sardonic sense of humor, often brazenly honest, and a quick wit with a slow drawl.

The other thing that would happen as he drank more was that he would sound more and more southern, (which he wasn't). This actually translated to sounding more black, however non-PC that term may sound today. He simply adored people of color. He dedicated much of his life to discovering, supporting and teaching young people of color. So it was only fitting that he and Arthur Mitchell—another great friend and special talent he had mentored—would be the co-founders of The Dance Theatre of Harlem. And it was he who was the catalyst for change as I moved on to study at DTH.

CHAPTER 6

BILLY'S BROADWAY

BILLY WILSON CHOREOGRAPHED eight musicals for the Broadway stage, one of which he also directed. *Bubbling Brown Sugar*, the all-black version of *Guys and Dolls*, and *Eubie!* were his most commercially successful shows, garnering him three Tony nominations.

Bubbling Brown Sugar was the show to revolutionize the representation of black performers on Broadway. This was the hit to put him permanently on the American map. With style, class and creative magic, he sprinkled brown sugar along The Great White Way. This was before *Ain't Misbehavin'*, before *Sophisticated Ladies* or *Black and Blue*. He was able to touch Broadway in a way that depicted African Americans in a positive light on stage. There were many questions for this new black choreographer on the Broadway scene, and he had plenty to say. When asked about where all of his diverse inspiration came from he replied, "As a black American, I don't feel restrained. I'm free to do anything from Bach to Beethoven, from blues to Basie." On the heels of Blaxploitation films and themes, Billy wanted to "create a sense of black chic. A feeling that, for once, we were celebrating ourselves."

Bubbling Brown Sugar was considered a musical review in two acts. It was a retrospective tour of Harlem spanning 1910 to present day. It included the compositions of Duke Ellington, Earl Hines and Billie Holiday. The cast starred Avon Long (the original Sportin' Life from Gershwin's *Porgy and Bess*), Thelma Carpenter (later replaced perhaps most notably by Josephine Premice), Vivian Reed and Joseph Attles. They were accompanied by the younger generation who were Danny Beard (played later by Chip Garnett), Ethel Beatty, Barbara Rubenstein and Barry Preston. The Chicago Daily News wrote: "The program credits identify him as the man responsible for choreography and musical staging; but in simple terms, it's safe to say that Billy Wilson is the man who put the bubbles in *Bubbling Brown Sugar*."

With the success of *Bubbling* came a steady knock at the door. The phones never stopped ringing with offers that kept him working and provided us with the comfort he so wanted us to enjoy. He had paid his dues and was beginning to reap the benefits of all his hard efforts. Without question, the challenge of having worked for Jerome Robbins on both *Bells Are Ringing* and *West Side Story* was at least partly responsible for helping him cut his teeth for bigger things on Broadway.

Frank Loesser's *Guys and Dolls* opened on Broadway in 1976 with my father's direction and choreography. This version starred Norma Donaldson, Robert Guillaume, Ernestine Jackson, and Jimmy Randolph, with a young Ken Page as Nicely-Nicely Johnson, who brought the house down each performance in "Sit Down, You're Rockin' the Boat."

The show was quite a challenge for my father. Because there was pressure to stay true to the original concept, he had writer Abe Burrows and the producers of the show breathing down his neck. He finally barred them from the rehearsals so that he could do the work without the added stress of their presence. In one interview, with both my father and Burrows, the author describes his job as, "Bothering Billy and things like that. The author is always at rehearsals." To which my father replied, "Until we get him out."

There was much controversy and speculation in the press about whether they could pull off an all-black version of the deliciously irresistible *Guys and Dolls*. If the shit hit the fan, Billy knew he would be the fall guy, and there were plenty of people looking for the black man in that historically white arena to fail. Thus, failing was not an option. He would go on to explain over and over again, in an effort to quell the nervous masses that, "We're not doing a take-off. This has good writing, good music, it's a good show. I'm involved in finding the honesty. People gamble. They fall in love. That isn't black or white. It's human." That show earned him his second Tony nomination for innovative staging and choreography

His third nominated show in succession was *Eubie!*, a musical tribute to the late, great Eubie Blake. However, the show was in trouble. Eight days before the first of two Philadelphia previews, the producers called my father in to save it—and save it he did. Unfortunately, after the work was done to the satisfaction of the producers and the critics, he spent the rest of the time fighting the producers for credit. The whole experience was messy and appallingly unfair. In the end he was fired—a move by the producers to save face and protect an incompetent director who rode on the coattails of Billy's clever and applauded work. Despite all the unnecessary drama, he garnered his third Tony nomination for work on that show. He would go on to choreograph four more shows for Broadway: *The Little Prince and the Aviator*, starring British film actor Michael York; *Dance a Little Closer*, by the prolific composer/lyricist Alan Jay Lerner; *Stop the World – I Want to Get Off*, starring Sammy Davis Jr.; and *Merlin*, starring the renowned magician Doug Henning and Broadway icon Chita Rivera.

In 1976, my father took me as his date to his first invitation as a nominee to the Tony Awards. Getting ready for that evening was very exciting, and naturally he'd bought me a special dress. It was a Cinderella night. Dad wore an Armani black tux with a very sharp black and white polka-dot bow tie. He added a splash of color with a blood-red pocket square. He looked incredibly handsome, the way he always looked to me. I was so proud of him and ecstatic to be on his arm that night. The evening was electrifying and the competition was stiff. It was, after all, Michael Bennett's year with *A Chorus Line*. He was the golden boy of the Great White Way and swept the Tonys. It didn't matter that my father didn't win that night, not to me anyway.

Although I would have expected remembering all of the famous faces around me, I don't recall a single one. That evening was reduced to a gentle pinprick of a thrilling night shared between my father and me. He had once again won my heart. At the end of the evening, after I'd drowsily unwrapped myself from all my creamy garments and gingerly extracted the bobby pins from my hair to let my braids fall, he smiled at me, and I hugged his tux-covered chest. It was where I wanted to remain forever. He was my hero. He'd rescued my brother and me from what I believe would have been a lesser life. That's perhaps putting it rather politely. If I'd stayed with my mother, I would have been a lot more fucked up. He loved us unconditionally and never passed up an opportunity to let us know it. I was a daughter in love with my father. I looked up at him with admiration. I hoped to grow up to be just like him. His love was like magic to me: magic off and on the stage.

On stage he was a dream of a choreographer, who also made more than 35 ballets for dance companies from The Alvin Ailey American Dance Theater to Opus 1 in Amsterdam, Holland. He made important contributions to the stage, created a reputation that never settled for less than 100 percent, and encouraged joy in an artist's approach to the work.

Backstage

Every morning Chip would wake before us and create whatever palatable delight we might desire—whatever might contribute to our being happy little children. After finishing our breakfast, we scrambled out into the wilderness of the city that we loved: Manhattan. It was the other half of what made growing up with my father magical. The bonus was being raised in and around show business.

My brother and I lived for the days we were allowed to be at auditions, in rehearsal studios, and finally in the theater. Our favorite projects happened during the summer months. That was when we could spend the entire sweltering New York day with our father while he did what he did best. We were especially excited going to the auditions for a new production. We spent those mornings into early evenings mostly laughing. Some performers came into the room and sincerely broke your heart with a ballad, while others raised the roof. But in the city, the fun was never knowing what might walk through that door.

Long before *American Idol* went public with its audition panel, we had a bird's-eye view all our own. There were always some certifiable nuts wearing exaggerated make-up, Halloween wigs, or a silver-sequined jumpsuit with go-go boots first thing in the morning. During those moments, we could hardly contain our hysterical outbursts and were then encouraged to go get a drink from the water fountain and stay a while. There were times when no one could keep a straight face and everyone would need a pee break to get composed again before the next entrance. We watched and cheered them on, knowing that these were determined souls who were pouring out their hearts and lives hoping for a big break.

At noon, there magically appeared an open cardboard box packed with an assortment of deli picks. Parker and I would usually choose a tuna sandwich or a BLT on white toast with potato chips and a dill pickle. The pickle juice always got a portion of the sandwich soppy. We wrinkled our noses, but it didn't stop us from devouring our delicious deli lunches. It was better than summer camp. We ate well and got to be entertained all day long!

My father took great pleasure in making the audition upbeat and comfortable for all those brave enough to show their stuff. I've never known anyone to really love auditioning, but everyone has to do it if they want that gig. What most performers do love is the opportunity to be hired to work hard at the thing they are passionate about doing: performing. Choosing a life in show business is not for the faint of heart. It takes a tough shell to get out there day after day; rejection after rejection; in the rain, sleet, or snow; year after year, chipping away at the chance for a chance. Auditioning for a job is a skill. Some are better at it than others.

Casting a show is an art. Discovering that diamond in the rough and deciding on that perfect performer for the part can make or break a show's success. This part of the process requires concentrated scrutiny and a dependable gut instinct for making the right choices about who will best serve the script, music, and choreography. The auditions also gave my father the chance to reconnect with old friends in the business he hadn't seen since a previous audition or past show. At some point during the week, someone of "priority" would arrive and be given extra-special treatment and handled with kid gloves in an effort to make him or her feel especially at ease. This was done out of respect and regard for the performer's work and fine reputation.

The next phase was the rehearsal period, and it provided new fun for us. Together with the director and musical arranger, we watched our father create and bring the concept to life. We didn't have to be asked too many times to stay put, because we sat in front of the mirrors transfixed by all that was going on, and we always felt welcome to be there with our father. At stolen moments, in between breaks, we would show Dad how we were learning the choreography, too.

The rehearsals were filled with sweat and high energy. Our father worked as if possessed, pressed by the element of time and driven by his creative juices to make something entertaining and exciting. We looked up at him with wonder and pride, while everyone else looked to him for approval and guidance. Perhaps it was in those rehearsal rooms that he became an even greater hero to me. I adored him all the more when I watched him paint his canvas, and it inspired me to dream.

The last stop was at the theater to get the show up and moving on the stage. This was when all the pieces came together to create another world. The costumes, sets, lights, music, dance and the powers that be decided what was still working and what wasn't. Being in the theater gave us a whole new physical freedom to fill up the space and explore while everyone else sweated it out to make magic. Like the love I felt from my father, the theater, too, was an undeniably magical place to spend a rainy afternoon.

While dancers slid in and out of their costumes to make their next entrance, we played hiding games, creeping up to the balcony and trying out every red crushed velvet seat in the theater or "house." As our father's stress level increased and we were reprimanded for making too much commotion, Parker and I would slip backstage to hang out in wardrobe, hair and make-up, or in the dressing room of our favorite cast member. I loved growing up in this way, surrounded by the lights, music, and movement of the the-ater. Those naturally sparkling moments shimmered all the more because we spent them with Daddy, who loved having us there. We also had the special privilege of coming in contact with some of the most talented and exciting people of the time.

Razzle dazzle

Four of those people, in particular, have always stood out in my mind as the most memorable and heart arresting. The first of those magnetic indi-viduals was Yul Brynner. I was with my father backstage at the Colonial Theater. It was this show, *The Odyssey*, starring Yul Brynner and Joan Diener, which brought my father from Boston to New York and the Broadway stage as a choreographer. The show itself was not memorable. In fact, it opened and closed almost simultaneously. However, my father's choreography and staging received positive reviews that were instrumental in kicking off his successful career in the commercial theater. I was nearing my eleventh birthday when he brought me to see the show.

I wore a floor-length sailor dress. The "maxi" was big for children dress-ing up in the '70s. My father had pulled my hair tightly back off my face and up high in a braided bun on top of my head. As always, he used Vaseline to ensure my hair would stay neat and shiny. I remember standing backstage in front of a floor mirror that seemed very old and somewhat distorted. Looking into that mirror, I suddenly saw a giant of a man standing behind my reflection. His overpowering figure took up all space in that mirror. Then I heard my father talking to him about me. He was introducing me when this larger-than-life man before me opened his mouth to speak.

The words came rolling out like great waves of a mystical sea, and I didn't know what to say. I realized I was in the presence of a very unusual being. I knew who Yul Brynner was from seeing *The King and I*, but meeting him took me off guard. I could only blink and blink and blink. I was familiar with the famous bald head, the open face, and gracefully folded Mongol eyes. He was simply a stunning and original creature. With all the aura of a god and with the voice of a mighty thundercloud, there was at once a gentle kindness and genuineness about him in his exchange with me.

Brynner and my father had become instantly attracted to one another as professionals, as artists, and as spiritual beings. My father told me over the years that Yul was one of his most treasured—albeit brief—friendships. He found him to be so down to earth—a man's man without a lot of bullshit. Their charisma and artistic reputations preceded their entrance into a room. He and my father held a strong sense of who they were and knew their worth. They found a kinship with one another and called each another "brother." I was simply in awe of Yul Brynner's gorgeous presence and feel so fortunate to have the physical and emotional memory of having been introduced to his uniqueness.

I also was introduced to Sarah Vaughan, aka Sassy, The Divine One. My father, Chip, Parker, and I were in London for six months while my father directed and choreographed *Irma La Douce*. Before beginning work on the musical, which would star Helen Gelzer and Charles Dance, he would stage Helen's act. Chip assisted him on both projects. This was the first time, of many, that I would see Sarah Vaughan live and in person. We grew up listening to her, the notes forever ringing through the rooms and hallways of the places we'd lived. From Antonio Carlos Jobim to Max Roach, from Tchaikovsky to Billie Holiday, we loved all kinds of music, but there was a special place in our hearts for Sarah. I could easily appreciate her vocal acrobatics and sass. She was a vocal marvel to me and I was ecstatic to hear and see her.

This time, I recall the hall being big and deep. She seemed far away. All was dark except for the special spotlight on her. She was covered with sparkles and sequins from head to toe—even shining in her hair. I was mesmerized. The song that stood out for me that evening was, of course, "Misty." How did she do that with her voice; start way up there in the rafters and effortlessly travel to the basement of her vocal range? She included some of the familiar licks, tricks and riffs that fans had grown to love. I jumped out of my seat with excitement, and the British were right there with me. After several encores, she left the stage again. The audience went mad and rushed the stage. It wasn't mass hysteria or frightening, but instead a dignified and orderly rush. They simply adored her and wanted to get closer to her. The footlights were very low to the ground and easily accessible. I moved quickly to the stage as well. It is one of the only times I have ever felt compelled in that way by an artist I was watching. I rushed, raced, ran down to the stage to reach out and touch the hand of that singing majesty. She found my fingers and brushed past.

I was thoroughly gleeful and satisfied. It was an evening never to be forgotten. I believe the excitement of that electric night helped to further my desire to be on that stage as well, drinking in all that applause, all that acceptance, and all that unabashed love. The thrill of her live performance had left me in love with Sarah Vaughan.

Sammy Davis Jr. was another indescribable talent who awed and inspired me. In 1978, my father was staging and choreographing *Stop the World – I Want to Get Off,* starring Davis and co-starring the very funny Marion Mercer. Mel Shapiro directed this production, which was created by Anthony Newley and Leslie Bricusse. Mel would later bring my father to Carnegie-Mellon University as an artist in residence. The show rehearsed and played in New York, with a limited run at Lincoln Center. There would also follow a film version—an awful version, I was told—that was rehearsed and shot in California.

My most vivid memory is of this little black man entering into a sun-flooded open rehearsal space in California. He had a nervous and jerky kind of walk. He came in wearing an oversized cream-colored T-shirt that hung almost to his knees over black pants. His hair was nearly standing straight up on his head. His thin neck was wound with numerous widths and lengths of gold that somehow gave balance to the assortment of gargantuan rocks and concoctions of gold and diamonds on his fingers. He made a small ceremony of taking off these various and sundry jewels, along with a tremendously large and exorbitant watch. He laid them squarely in the center of the table where Mel and my father sat. A couple of quick jokes were exchanged and he was ready to begin.

He took a few awkward steps back and opened his mouth wide to let the whole host of angels in heaven and earth fill the room. It was a gift of song that rendered everyone in the room speechless. The size and beauty of the voice that came from this little unlikely looking man were none other than a gift given by a supreme force. It, and he, were just extraordinary. Once again, I knew I was in the presence of something not only great but also very rare. And there was so much more to this talent than the voice. The voice was one of the seven wonders, but his talents were endless. There were his gun tricks, his drumming, his impressions, his tapping—and the list went on. He shared a little bit of everything with the cast during the rehearsal period.

Some drama and fatigue also accompanied the superstar. My father would say that Sammy was often as incorrigible and exasperating as he was beloved and charming. When the nature of the talent is truly great, people have the capacity for putting up with an awful lot. This man's story was so astounding—growing up a baby in show business with no schooling and self-taught since age nine, being on the road, facing racism, living the Rat Pack days, falling in love with and marrying white women in the public eye during a fiercely segregated era—and his "protectors," who kept the bottles stocked with soda water instead of the hard stuff.

I am most fond of my memory of watching my father watch Sammy. Sammy had been one of the true superstars of his generation. He was also one of a handful of black performers—among them Lena Horne, Louis Armstrong and Paul Robeson—who had made international careers. They had all blazed the trail for the next generation to have faith in their dreams of succeeding.

My father had grown up in awe of this superman. Now he had the honor and responsibility of having Sammy Davis Jr. look to him for guidance and reassurance. I would watch my father watching Sammy, and it warmed my heart to see him gazing up at him in wonder, like a little boy. To be working with a real god of the theatre and with the musical talent this giant possessed was a dream come true for my father. My brother and I also watched, listened, and tried to learn a little something from this legend in our midst. We were young but we recognized the weight of the experience.

LITTLECHAP was the name of Sammy's character in the show, and the staging that my father created for him and his small frame was just delicious. I loved watching a show and its cast come together. Although only an adolescent, I sensed this cast seemed genuinely connected to one another. There is almost always a bond that develops when putting on a production together. It comes from the sheer nature of working hard and closely to create something from nothing.

However, some productions suffer from a difference of vision or a clash of egos, which can breed lifelong dissention among cast members and often create enemies. Some have destroyed a career or two along the way and ruined reputations in an incestuous business where word of mouth can get you the gig or get you fired before you've even auditioned.

But this production, along with all the expected drama, seemed to create camaraderie and good feelings. My father expressed to me that there were instances with Sammy that were a bit upsetting. He recognized the star's need to show a public display of appreciation and respect to white people surrounding him, in particular, while glaringly reluctant to extend that same courtesy to my father. Those moments were hurtful and disappointing, but they didn't outweigh the admiration my father felt when watching the genius that was Sammy Davis Jr.

The one and only time I came face to face with another living legend was when I was with my father attending a performance of something that I do not recall. However, getting the opportunity to meet this great lady stayed with me. It was the only recollection of that evening.

My father professed, along with the multitudes, that he had always had a crush on Lena Horne. This came as an eye-opener to me because up until that point, I'd only heard about how everyone had a crush on him. The crush became all too real when he was hired as a dancer in 1957 to join the company of the Broadway show *Jamaica,* in which she starred with Ricardo Montalban.

She was one of a handful of black talents to pave the way and gracefully slice her way into the itchy palm of the money-hungry establishment called Hollywood. She was a seemingly untouchable movie star who nonetheless remained in touch with the world and let her voice be heard in the midst of the civil rights movement. Her own stories of surviving discrimination and racism were a testament to her strong will and courage. Behind this stunning and talented beauty was her determination to not only survive but also to thrive! She often played the Hollywood game her way, and though the reaction to her being "straight ahead" was sometimes shocking to those who looked for this pretty light-skinned gal to be grateful and accommodating, she seemed unshakable in her need to be true to who she was. This was the Lena Horne I came to know from a distance and grew to so ardently admire.

One of my great disappointments was never having seen her one-woman Broadway show *Lena Horne: The Lady and Her Music*. To this day I don't know how I missed it. My father and Chip saw this "magical and electrifying experience" over and over again. The opening night of that show has gone down in history as one of the truly great nights of theater. Soon after that missed magic, I vowed to see her live before one of us left this planet.

My father's feelings for Ms. Horne, as performer and as mere mortal, were different from those he held for anyone else. He had seen the gamut of live artistry, from Judy Garland to Josephine Baker to Charles Aznavour, but I believe it was Lena Horne who most inspired and excited him. One of his favorite recollections of her during the run of *Jamaica* was her metamorphic witch-like change from the ordinary into a superhuman, super-kinetic, super-knockout, take-no-prisoners performer who raised the roof and left the audience gasping for air.

It wasn't until many years later that my father spotted her sitting across the aisle from us during a performance I can't remember. When it was over, he brought me over to meet her. She seemed so small, even meek. She was on the arm of a gentleman who seemed to be of great support, and although the introduction and exchange was brief, it was perfection. Meeting her in that way, as just the woman, made the moment all the sweeter. It was, after all, not the regalia that made her who she was. That was part of the performer. It was more thrilling and special to feel that I'd met the person. I felt so proud knowing it was through the history of my father's experience with her that had made meeting her an easy possibility. I felt honored to be slipping that piece of history into my evening purse to save for a rainy day, to share with my children, or simply to hold and cherish.

The journey with my father and his work was made so special because my brother and I got a peek, over and over again, into the working lives of these great talents. We were not only watching them perform from the wings or out front in full make-up, under the right lights, and in exquisite costumes.

We saw them sweat, struggle with the note, forget the dialogue, wrestle with the costume that wasn't working, and then laugh out loud at the jokes and the insanity of it all. We bore witness to the process that made meeting these gods and goddesses of the theater so beautiful. To watch them as imperfect beings battling their own demons made the journey rich and human.

And in the work, it was my father's humanness that had a lot to do with bringing that trust out into the open and creating an environment that helped these supremely gifted and often complicated beings feel comfortable, confident, and safe on the stage. It was not too unlike the way my father made me feel.

Style, Baby!

Broadway choreographer and tap dancer extraordinaire Maurice Hines, likes to tell a story about the first time the company of *Eubie!* met Billy Wilson and Chip Garnett. The show was in rehearsal, but it was in trouble. My father was hired to take over and create his own choreography but essentially ended up directing as well. The company members were all assembled when my father and Chip made quite the entrance. Maurice told me that no one expected that my father was actually there to rehearse, as he was *dressed* and coordinated from head to toe. Chip was no exception. My father began by announcing that there was very little time to get the show together and because of that he said, "The word for today is *retain*." There was no time for anything else. It was pure Billy. He came in with guns blazing ready to work, but he was going to do it looking sharp and with tremendous style.

Billy had a wonderful mix of being in step with current fashion but always with a touch of European classic *splash*. In the fall, I can still see him walking confidently, kicking his turned-out feet in front of him. It was a kind of hanging back walk that many dancers, especially ballet dancers have; they sit back in their legs. It is undeniably a dancer's walk: a beautifully familiar walk. He possessed an ease that can only come from years of experience, of paying dues, of being successful and simply tossing it respectfully away. I loved his walk, his stroll. I loved the "no-need-to-impress" in his walk. It was confidence, not arrogance. He would say, "Own it! If *you* don't believe it no one else will." But that walk was unmistakably Billy Wilson's.

I picture him in olive green, thick-ribbed relaxed-fitting cords, those really wide mushy cords, with a butter cream-yellow turtleneck in that nice soft plush cotton that hung on the outside past his waist, and an expensive watch. His last favorite watch was a silver and gold Cartier. It was understated but it still made a statement. He would always say, "Less is more."

In keeping with his monochromatic daywear, he might sport his olive suede safari jacket wrapped around his waist and complete the look with a baseball cap of beige or khaki. Big, wide, dark tortoise-shell sunglasses with a square shape, and on his fingers, blinding flashes of elegant bands with diamonds and emeralds. He always wore a little bit of tasteful bling. He loved jewelry, and his was always masculine and refined. He usually carried some kind of shoulder bag that held his reading glasses, Chap Stick, hairbrush for his short cut, phonebook, and other small necessities. These were things that helped to keep him in touch and to keep his unapologetic vanity intact. He kept his billfold in his right back pocket.

Both my father and Chip loved to shop. They were clotheshorses and enjoyed it. The two of them were also humorously and lovingly competitive with their clothing collections. They especially loved Brown's of London and the Kalvestraat in Amsterdam. Any opportunity to shop in either city or any great shopping city, for that matter, gave them giddy pleasure. Anyone who knew Billy and Chip almost instantly gets a mental picture of these two handsome, confident, and beautifully put-together men. As they grew together, their tastes, feelings, and thoughts were so interlaced they would often dress in their separate rooms only to discover before walking out the door that they had dressed almost identically. We would all fall out laughing. There would be a pause for a humorous standoff, and invariably Chip would defer to my father's seniority. Saying, "Age before beauty," he would end up changing his ensemble entirely. Those were terrifically funny and endearing moments and ones when my agitation with Chip would temporarily be forgotten. The two of them loved their "drag" and enjoyed the pleasure that buying nice things brought them. However, my father, in particular, was not confused or under any illusion about the significance of material things.

There's a line from the movie *Julia* that he loved. Dashiell Hammett (Jason Robards) and Lillian Hellman (Jane Fonda) are sitting on the beach at night talking about her work that's recently been hailed a success. She tells him she'd like to buy a sable coat. He replies, "If you want a sable coat, buy one. Just remember, it doesn't have anything to do with writing. It's only a sable coat and doesn't have anything to do with writing." My father used to say that it's important to enjoy your moments but equally important not to forget whom you are and what got you there. I believe he loved most of his work and the fruits of his labor. Together with the added knowledge that he'd always 'worked his behind off,' as he would say, made that enjoyment all the sweeter.

He took great care in his home. He was a self-professed homebody when he wasn't in a rehearsal room or at the theater. He cherished being at home and the comfort of always knowing that there you can truly shed your skin and be yourself. He loved cleaning the apartment and keeping things looking fresh. His home and his love of it were as big a part of who he was as his other passions. He liked things in place without being austere. He wanted the vibe to be welcoming and relaxed. When friends would visit, they were sometimes loath to plop down on the perfectly fluffed sofa for fear of disturbing the lovely scene. However, it was one of the first places he encouraged a guest to relax. We didn't have visitors all the time, primarily because he so valued his downtime. It was for him a real treat not having to be "on" and full of endless inspiration and super-hero energy.

In the apartment he slid into his well-worn royal-blue terry slippers and a short terry robe to match. When the weather was warmer, he'd lounge around with the top half of that blue robe down to hang around his hips. I think of that robe worn in that way and other memories leap to mind. I see him bent over the tub scrubbing away or on the floor working the black and white tiles with a bucket of hot water and Ajax. On his hands and knees, this familiar choreography would bring the satisfaction of glistening cleanliness to the surface of his patterned masterpiece.

He garnered tremendous satisfaction from these household chores. I can remember Parker and me laughing when he'd be up vacuuming, sometimes as early as 7:00 a.m. on Saturdays. As kids, we would be so evil waking to the *vrooooooom* of the vacuum cleaner. We called him Joan (for Joan Crawford in *Mommie Dearest*). I would say, "You're funny, Dad" and he'd reply, "Yeah, you're funny too ... but you see this rug is flawless, don't you?" We couldn't argue with that. We'd laugh hard and he'd go right on dusting or cleaning mirrors. He'd say, "I love clean!" He told us cleaning was his therapy, and as much as I laughed at him, it gradually became my therapy as well. He told me he got it from his mother. I believe these things helped to keep him grounded. One could see him in all his beautiful vanity at home, arranging flowers in our small New York kitchen and singing, "Forget your troubles, come on, get happy." He was happy. When friends came to visit, they were dear to his heart and it would be hours of great talk and delicious food that Chip would prepare with great flourish, and rolling-on-the-floor laughter.

He had a heightened sense of the beauty around him. He adored and appreciated all things beautiful, whether beautiful flowers—one of his favorite pleasures—beautiful clothes, beautiful bodies, beautiful bedclothes, beautiful music to listen to or beautiful dancers to be mesmerized by. All these beauties were like oxygen to his heart and soul. These things kept him young, vibrant, creative, and thriving. He taught me the magic and wonder of discovering beauty in the simplest of things.

I recall a time when he put a tape into the player and said, "Listen to this. You'll love this Holly; it's Mahler's *Fifth*." I listened and was immediately swept away. As the music unfolded, he took me on a journey. He painted the picture for me. He saw the sun rising in the music. I closed my eyes. I was right there with him as the sun broke and settled over stillness in the musical phrase. He brought me to what the colors were and where they danced across a fantastic landscape. He then asked, "Can you see that?" I told him yes, I did see it. The journey was complete. He had painted for me the beginning, middle, and end. It was profoundly beautiful and important to my life experience with my father. I never forgot the moment of listening to that gorgeous piece of music with him.

Billy's style was grand, not small; elegant, and not ostentatious. He was about being in the moment; enjoying fun and intelligent company, engaging conversation, savoring splendid food, delighting in the deliciousness of nature, being excited by youth, respectful of experience, in awe of great masters of anything, loving "the work," appreciating real friendships, forever falling in love, possessing the wonder of a child and bathing in the precious wealth of having children. His style was drinking in life. He did it with grace, honesty, imperfection and great humanity.

Wonderful, how after all these years the important endearing particulars come eagerly to the surface. His dress and style; the manner in which he carried himself was an important and beautiful part of all that went into making Billy Wilson father, often mother, provider, teacher, choreographer, director, artist, and human being. His charm was irresistible and his flair irrepressible. He was never afraid of color, never afraid of being unique and somehow always escaped being "off" in his choice of what worked for him. To me, he was undeniably masculine. On some other man, a certain something might have taken on a costumed effect. With Chip I caught elements of femininity and even slightly effeminate at times, but not with my father. Perhaps this was just a daughter's need to keep her father's masculine image intact, but I don't think so. I think my perception was correct, despite my also wanting things to be regular or "normal." My acceptance of many things didn't always come easily.

CHAPTER 7

CUTTING TEETH

WHEN I WAS young, standing at the ballet barre, my father would place his hand on my lower back to give me support as he gently nudged my leg to go higher. As it inched closer and closer to the tip of my nose, he would gradually let go, and it was my job to hold it there. "Hold it, hold it," he'd say. I'd inhale, give my leg a last push upward before he'd say, "a-n-d let it go." Always higher, always more, but even more important, what was I saying with it? What purpose or story lay behind the need for me to be up there dancing? He was interested in the point of view. *Where have you been? Where are you going?* It was the same thing one might ask an actor: *What do you want in this scene?*

He was as excited as the next person by a dancer, singer or actor's technical ability, but bored easily if that was all. It was a novelty quick to wear off with him. He would say, "But where's the juice?" He was forever reminding me, as well as his students, that there would always be someone cuter, prettier, quicker, or smarter. The bigger question was, "What will you do with it while you've got it? What makes you more special than the other twenty girls waiting in the wings, and what will you do when the *icing* is gone?"

He was speaking of longevity and what it takes to build a career. He grew up always looking at the ways in which one had to be constantly reinventing and sustaining oneself, particularly as an artist. Working with Billy, as I sometimes playfully called him, was a wonderful experience, but also filled with pressure. When I began dancing professionally, he often used me to work out new pieces of choreography, especially when creating a pas de deux. The blessing and the challenge was in his being both father and teacher. I sometimes found it a struggle to find a harmonious balance between the two. He believed that struggle was inside my head and not anything that he was creating—not consciously anyway. However, there could never be a total separation between work and our deeper roles. It made the journey more interesting, made the stakes higher, the challenges richer, and the falls harder. The night before a rehearsal with him was exciting and charged with "good" energy. The day of the rehearsal, I was anxious and filled with fear of not doing my best. He would ask me why I put myself through such anxiety; although I tried to explain myself, it always seemed difficult for him to fathom. I naturally wanted to please him and the weight of living up to his expectation was not always easy. Despite that tall order of expectation, one of the things I greatly respected was his ability to be fair. Whether it was a young man who'd just walked into his rehearsal from the street or me, that fairness was based on a person's individual potential. He especially did not pander to my personal dramas or self-indulgence where the work was involved.

While still a young teen, I worked with him on a PBS special called *Blues and Gone*. It was a collection of vignettes of dance to the music of Duke Ellington, among others, inspired by the poems of Langston Hughes. The special earned him an Emmy. He and Chip conceptualized it, wrote it, and Chip, Parker and I performed it, along with five other dancers. This project was very close to his heart, and he had assembled some of his favorite talents. Although my brother and I were excited to be a part of our father's project, I nearly got myself fired. He believed in nepotism, but not at the expense of the work. There was a lot of laughter and fun when working with him but when the time came to get to it, he had no time for B.S. I might have been his daughter, but I still had to deliver. You could be the cutest thing to walk through the door but if you weren't makin' it or if you weren't able to rise to the occasion, you were out! On the PBS project there was the added element of *time is money*.

There I was, in the middle of puberty (part of the problem), with legs as long as the Mississippi River, facility as easy as running water, and with a disposition as sour as a freshly squeezed lime. I was not the picture of *grateful to be there*. I spent most of my adolescence being angry at the world. It was mostly the upheaval of our family—and more specifically the disappearance of my mother—that never allowed me to trust fully the longevity of happiness. I always felt that a great disappointment was just around the bend.

Up until the time we started filming, I had just been going through the motions; dancing my solo adequately but with no real energy. When I wasn't needed, I was supposed to be learning whatever was being done. Instead, I would get lazy and dreamy. Fortunately, I was working for the man who knew me better than anyone. He knew what I could do, should do, and needed to do if I wanted to be more than just another dancer with high legs and pretty feet.

He let me go for a while. But one day he pulled me aside. "Holly, you've got about five minutes to pull yourself together," he said, "or I'm going to have to find someone else to do your part. If you don't want to take advantage of this opportunity and start dancing with some joy and energy, then you can save us both a lot of time and aggravation and give someone who would love to be doing what you're doing and getting paid for it, the opportunity. You're my daughter and I love you, but I don't have time for this. Everyone is working very hard and excited to be here but you. So what's the problem?"

I said nothing. I was stunned. He got me. He went on, "You're only cheating yourself. And you're not doing it for me because I've done it. I've had the dance career; it's your turn, *if* you decide you want it badly enough. I won't always be there to push you." I was caught and I was embarrassed because I was failing him. I didn't want to do that. I pulled it together and began working at the level that I should have from the very beginning.

I learned a lot from my *Blues and Gone* experience and continued to learn, particularly when I found myself revisiting that counterproductive pattern. I learned that I had a pretty good deal having a father who knew a thing or two about achieving the thing that I hoped to one day achieve. I learned that if I stayed open to his wisdom and to the process, I could be better. I was touching the tip of the iceberg in realizing that the world did not revolve around me and in fact could go on quite easily without me. I was learning that pretty legs and feet do not a great dancer make, that one part of something affects the whole, and that one negative element has the potential to spoil it for everyone. In hindsight, I'm grateful to have had a father who not only made it possible for me to display my talents but also had the where-withal to be honest with his child about the business of it all.

I straddled between being two people for two different functions. On the one hand, I felt I had it easy because I *was* Billy Wilson's daughter and could therefore hang back and take a lot for granted. On the other hand, I needed to work twice as hard to prove myself *because* I was his daughter. I had to especially fight my comfort zones, the places where things did come more easily for me physically. What came easily could be a trap if not used properly.

Seasoned artists like my father, Karel, choreographer Louis Johnson, and Arthur Mitchell often said they were astonished that over and over again that those with the greatest natural gifts were the ones left in the dust, replaced by those who had to sweat blood for every small milestone they earned. They were sometimes the ones who forged on ahead to become the trailblazers. They were often more hungry and more passionate with a single-minded determination to conquer the thing.

If you were someone who came along hungry, my father shared with you that insatiable appetite. He would work with you, help you, and guide you. If he felt you weren't serious or were too self-indulgent, he would move on to the next starving artist in line—someone who was eager for the challenge and unafraid of the hard work. He shared all of that with me, as well as the showbiz stories and trivia.

He talked about his experience dancing in *West Side Story* in London. He got a pure thrill watching Chita Rivera burn up the stage each night! He also said that Jerome Robbins, the iconic ballet and Broadway choreographer, was "a perfect monster to the dancers, especially if he didn't like you. He would make your life miserable; saying the most awful and personal things to a person to make him or her want to shrivel away."

He recalled an instance that turned into a very unfortunate day of thanks. Billy had plans for Thanksgiving. His time away had been okayed with the powers that be. It wouldn't be a long trip, but it was a chance to at least spend the holiday with his family back in Philly. Robbins knew of his plans but the night before departure, he called a rehearsal that required my father's presence. The next morning, Billy brought his luggage with him to rehearsal, planning to leave immediately after he was done being used. The minutes turned into hours and the hours turned into a full day of not being used at all. Consequently, he missed his train and never did get home to Philadelphia that Thanksgiving.

Although the situation might have been deliberately unfair, he took from it another valuable lesson: that these often difficult circumstances, the forks in the road demanded of artists, are the very moments that separate the men from the boys. It is the nature of the beast and par for the course. Being an artist is not all glamour or bohemian bliss. It comes with a cost. The unfair and upsetting situations and choices, along the way, come disguised as greater life lessons. Those moments were defining and instrumental in carving out my father's character and commitment to that which he claimed to be passionate about. What he took from it was, "It's preparing me for my greater work." He had grown from his life lessons. It was time for me to start doing the same.

Enjoying the process

At that age and stage in my development and education, I felt anything I'd learned of any real value came from listening, watching, and soaking up all that Billy had to offer as father and as teacher. He taught me the beauty of the creative process. He'd say. "That's where the 'meat' is—figuring it out, making big mistakes, taking chances! Enjoy the process."

I learned by watching him work through his own process in the rehearsal rooms. He could be tough and demanding but always with positive reassurance and with belief in the possibility of what you could achieve. He wasn't into berating, throwing chairs or demeaning you. He worked fast and didn't believe in too much counting or too much conversation. He didn't fall for tears, but was genuinely concerned if he knew you needed extra support. If someone came to the process with a negative vibe or a truculent attitude, he called it out and nipped it in the bud.

He was about your challenging yourself, daring you to think bigger and give yourself over to the work. Part of what made Billy a great teacher— not just a good one—was that *the work* really became a metaphor for *your life*. While you learned something through the work, you were also learning more about who you were and your place in the world. It came in the form of choices you made about your character, the way in which you chose to work, the space and grace you extended to him and the artists with whom you worked, your strengths, and your shortcomings. His scope was never provincial. It was expansive and international. For him, the creative process had to be uplifting and positive. He joked, laughed, and believed in enjoying the process, but he came to *work*. He expected you to do the same. He sometimes made fun of me for taking myself too seriously.

Artists and performers, in general, loved working with Billy. He inspired them to work with a lot of energy as he demonstrated the choreography or direction, dancing and acting circles around the young men and women ten to twenty years his junior. He would say, "You young people need to fluff! Where's all that youthful energy? I've got more energy than all you children and I'm old enough to be your grandfather, for God sakes! Work with me, people! We've got about five minutes before we're in the theater." He wanted you to get it.

Billy Wilson was a dancer first, and he understood the fragility of artists. He handled artists with love and care but he didn't baby sit nor did he have too much patience for what he called "dumb-de-dumb-dumb," also known as "not too bright." Spending two weeks of rehearsal with someone who still wasn't getting the step or the dialogue was a potential problem for everyone. If he had to, he'd pull you out. That was the "business" in show business, and he understood it very well. It was all of these qualities that made working through the process and being taught by Billy Wilson so exceptional. Aside from the occasional struggles with myself while working for my father, the times spent with him were precious.

A particular quality I relished watching was his effortless ability to become the moment. He had no fear or self-consciousness in that way. If he needed a woman to walk across the stage, put her foot up on top of a garbage can and straighten her stockings with *heat*, he would demonstrate. He became that woman and wore the role like a second skin. If he needed a brute, full of piss and vinegar, with flexing macho muscles, he would become that, too. These transformations came to him with such easy conviction you believed this ability was in your grasp as well. He wanted you to possess it and make it your own: to glorify it. He helped me to surrender to the process and enjoy the journey and its perils. In a spiritual way, he believed that it was your responsibility not to squander or take for granted the gifts given to you by God.

Joining ranks

It was through my godfather, Karel Shook that I was given the opportunity to study at the Dance Theater of Harlem as an apprentice. That meant I would be on payroll. I was thirteen years old and very excited. My objective, when I decided I wanted to become a dancer, was to become a "great" dancer, the very best at anything I set out to accomplish. This credo I attribute largely to my father's teaching, though I am certain my mother felt the same way. It was a conviction of succeeding strongly connected to an African American way of life growing up. This was an important ingredient in the mission statement that Arthur Mitchell and The Dance Theatre of Harlem was founded upon. It was this powerful energy and these living and breathing dancing examples who would help to foster my inner conviction about who I was and who I wanted to become.

It was 1978 and DTH was unique and internationally recognized. To be a member of this primarily black ballet company was very exciting. I also had the support and guidance of people who loved me, namely Karel, Arthur Mitchell, and Lorraine Graves (the former ballet mistress of the company), among others. Mr. Mitchell was a very important force in my life, both professionally and personally. He continuously pushed me—like Richard Thomas before him—challenged my abilities, and offered me the opportunity to shine. He was tough on dancers because he expected only their very best. Personally, he was yet another positive male influence on both my brother and me. He, too, kept an extra eye on us and helped us stay on the straight and narrow. It takes a village and the village isn't always composed only of women.

Mr. Mitchell always encouraged us and held us accountable for our choices and the decisions we were making as young adults. It was especially exciting to have him both in the rehearsal studio and as the occasional visitor to our home. He and my father would reminisce about the past and plan projects together. Aside from Mr. Mitchell and Karel Shook, DTH was responsible for giving me the very best training and discipline possible, which included dance legends like Mary Hinkson and Tanaquil LeClercq. That was the next ingredient that added to my foundation and would serve me for the rest of my life. I was grateful and recognized from the beginning the importance and significance of this gift that I had been granted. I would receive my weekly stipend as an apprentice member as long as I maintained a B average.

For four years, Parker and I attended Professional Children's School. We took the subway each morning to school on the Broadway local from 110th Street to Columbus Circle. The school allowed me to work largely by correspondence since I was needed for classes and rehearsals all day. At P.C.S., we entered a social epicenter and a very protected environment. All of the pro theatrical kids went there, from an adolescent Diane Lane to James Bond the III, little Peter Billingsly, Martha Plimpton, and Sarah Jessica Parker, who'd just landed the role of Annie on Broadway to follow Andrea McArdle and would later become a friend of mine before becoming the iconic Carrie Bradshaw.

One of the only things I actually learned at that school was how to sing harmony parts and how *not* to walk like a ballet dancer. There were young up-and-coming dancers like Darci Kistler from New York City Ballet and Peter Boal, who was in my class. They would later become big ballet stars. Many DTH star dancers had also attended P.C.S., including Virginia Johnson and my contemporary rising starlet Thera Ward. There was quite a gaggle of pretty dancers, each one walking more turned out than the next. Even though I'd been born into a world into which nearly everyone around me walked like that, for some reason I did not want to be recognized by that trademark. I decided I would walk turned in. Dancers walked like ducks. I would walk like a pigeon.

By the age of fourteen, I was spending my days largely out of school and in rehearsals. During the performing season, I spent the evenings dancing in the corps de ballet at City Center. I was dancing in *The Four Temperaments* by George Balanchine, *Serenade* by Balanchine, *Dougla* by Geoffrey Holder and the occasional *Swan Lake*.

After the curtain came down one evening, all of us were still milling on stage. Friends and family would come back to meet with us, give us hugs, kisses, and bouquets of carnations mixed with violets and soft pink roses. On this one particular evening, I was introduced to an incredibly important person, Ms. Cicely Tyson. She'd been a longtime supporter and friend of DTH, Mr. Mitchell, and our family friend Lorenzo James. She also knew my father and Chip. Ms. Tyson is a true queen of the theater, of film, and of the craft. She is a living legend and one of the most elegant ladies in the business. She has been a trailblazer and an inspiration to so many people of color, especially to the young aspiring artists, as I was when I met her.

She came over to me and spoke softly and gently, telling me I had a special gift and talent to share. She offered her encouragement that I continue to nurture it, own it, and use it. I didn't say a word, but just listened as she ended by telling me that if I should ever need something, I should find her. I have always remembered her kindness and the sincere words she spoke to me. Once again I was graced with having met one of the truly great artists of our time. That evening ended, the next morning showed up, and I began all over again to work, work, and work.

At the time I loved what I was doing—and getting paid for it—but I had a hard time juggling my schoolwork with dancing demands. There were those like Thera Ward, Carol Crawford, and Terri Tompkins, all apprentices then, who seemed to sail through their studies to maintain their B average. In all honesty, they probably just worked extremely hard to do what was necessary. I was maintaining a D or C—when I was lucky. It was such a scary thing to go into Mr. Mitchell's office to talk about grades, even though I had a closer relationship with him than most. Nepotism didn't protect me then. I had always found it hard to apply myself in school, except for those subjects that held a real interest for me. I wanted a life with my friends, outside of DTH. In essence, I wanted to hang out more. Unfortunately, it's difficult to become a great dancer *and* hang out more. This ambivalence led to my leaving DTH more than once before leaving for good. Transitions were once again afoot, and they included a physical move meant to bring us all closer together.

CHAPTER 8

FRESH START

W E NEEDED OUR own rooms. Parker also needed to run around more to nurture his budding athletic talents. My father needed a good tax move, and the idea of living in the suburbs, without the constant buzz of the city, became more and more appealing to him. He felt that, especially for us, living in a house again would give us back some of the stability, familiarity, and comfort we'd left behind since the separation on West Brookline Street. He wanted to reclaim those lost feelings that said "home."

He also knew it would be a dream come true for Chip: the life he'd always wanted. Chip was ecstatic, Parker was excited, my father was optimistic, and I was miserable. Parker loved the idea of a new adventure. I, a bona fide teenager by that time in love with the energy of the city, and with all my friends being there, saw no point in a move. Granted, it would be nice to have our own rooms again. As beautiful and spacious as the apartment had been, it was nonetheless a two-bedroom place. Parker and I had been sharing a trundle bed in what was actually a maid's room off the kitchen. As tiny as it was, it still felt better than living with my mother.

I will never forget that tiny blue room. It was our vessel of transition from one world to another. The walls were the color of a blue Papermate pen:

slate grey with a hint of deep turquoise. The color was not too unlike the apartment on the Charles River in Boston. Not the most beautiful shade of blue. These sordid variations on a theme of blues seemed a repeating pattern that followed us through the murkiness of challenging times. It seemed the metaphor representing where I often found myself ... waking up in blue. Not the crisp clear blue of the Mediterranean waters or what one gets lost in while gazing into Big Sky country, but a sad hue. However, the shade had begun to transform, gradually taking on more light and less load if I would allow it. But in that little room sat only a twin bed with the rail we pulled up to bring the hidden twin out from under it, a small narrow rectangular window, a half-bath with a showerhead craned stiffly over it, and a toilet that was never used. It was temporary and that was fine.

Apart from the fact that all was not smooth between Chip and me, we were warm and safe with our father. Since I was pretending I was not affected by the absence of my mother, Chip was then the only caveat in this new big ball of wax. Our mother had given us up to our father, and I was now faced with the person I fervently believed was my nemesis. If ever I thought, while in the apartment, that perhaps he would tire of us and leave, all hopes were dashed with the new plan of moving into a house altogether.

Not perfect

It was hard to warm to Chip because of his determination to please and to be accepted. Yet weren't we all just trying for that same thing? My father was seeking acceptance from his children, especially me; acceptance of his lifestyle; and acceptance from the white Broadway establishment as a bona fide choreographer. I was trying to gain acceptance from my friends by shutting *out* my home life, and Parker sought it from anyone who was willing to make up for the lack of a mother. And our mother went about filling the void where her family had once been with anything *but* her family.

However, Chip's particular eagerness to win me over was simply fuel for my hateful fire. I had become so hell-bent on staying angry, I was becoming an absolute horror to live with. Aside from Chip's being a fiercely talented singer, dancer, actor and cook, he was also the kind of person who excelled at everything he set out to accomplish. Whatever he touched, even on his first attempt, seemed to work and come together as if he'd always done it. His right brain and his left brain worked exceedingly well. He was as gifted at problem solving with numbers as he was at creating a delectable Thanksgiving spread. He was exceptional at cooking everything from duck a l'orange with a chef's presentation to baking triple-layer strawberry shortcake from scratch with gluttonous amounts of fresh whipped cream. He made this cake for me year after year on my birthdays. And though I resented his loving efforts, I gobbled without pause. He was an overachiever, a do-gooder, and a seemingly "perfect" person. I used to call him "Mr. Perfect," though to me he would never come close to perfect. But he never stopped trying.

Chip wanted so much to make us feel loved and cared for that he taught himself how to make children's clothes. He would come home from an audition or rehearsal with patterns for dresses and tops for me. He would sew them expertly on his brand-new sewing machine. Years later he would design luxurious plush terry bath robes for friends, which led to a line sold by Charivari, Henri Bendel's, and Bloomingdale's. I rejected each of his prodigious talents. Though I ate his food and wore the clothes he'd made for me, I did so grudgingly. I wanted nothing to do with his gifts, his show of affection, or his love for me. In fact, the harder he tried, the more I hated him for it.

Everything about him got under my skin. The way he smiled, the way he moved, his grandeur, and the feeling that I got from him of being slightly condescended to and judged, were all bits of a whole that added only up to negatives in my mind. Of course, he told my father everything. Nothing seemed safe within his earshot. I had a vague sense that Chip thought he was "better than" because he was smart and wore it like a badge. In a lot of ways, it was probably his smarts that saved him from many racist and complicated situations. His intelligence and his talent had won him awards and scholarships. It also helped shield him from other people's scrutiny about how difficult his upbringing had been.

I didn't know a lot about his past, and it wasn't a subject he talked about. I knew he was born in Gary, Indiana. He had at least four siblings, three of whom I'd met over the years. His mother had three of the children with different men. I believe it was he and his sister Kim who had the same father. I don't remember ever hearing him mention his father. I don't know if he'd ever even known him. His mother had a tough time keeping it together, so Chip, the eldest, helped raise his younger siblings while still a child himself. He cooked, cleaned, got the other children ready for school in the mornings, while his mother remained challenged simply to be clear and accountable. He continued to assume the mother role up until college.

As a child, Chip's fast brain and musical talent set him apart. In school he was "different" and teased for acting "white" and being bookish. He loved to learn, received high marks in all his subjects, and received special attention from his teachers. He went on to attend Indiana University on scholarship. By that time he was singing whenever he could. He got involved with drama and musical theater, and that's when he got bitten by the high of being on stage. He had a girlfriend in college, but it didn't last long. Later he would tell me, "She was sweet, but it didn't feel right." He soon made his way to New York City in search of the vehicle to get him onto the Broadway stage. First he got off-Broadway ensemble work. Then in 1973, he joined the cast of *Inner City* and soon thereafter made his Broadway debut among the impressive cast of Harold Prince's *Candide.* Bit by bit he was getting work and gaining credibility as a voice worth listening to and hiring. The year 1976 brought him a lead role in *Bubbling Brown Sugar* and he just kept wanting more. Chip loved being on stage receiving the waves of love that applause carried past the footlights. I think that unconditional appreciation and acceptance were the feelings that he was in search of.

To the outside world he laughed grandly, he shopped expensively, and spoke with an almost booming confidence. He loved champagne and rich desserts. My father was happy to help provide Chip with a lot of work, either as performer or as his assistant on various projects. They often conceived original projects together. However, not too unlike the scenario of many women, when the domestic move to the suburbs happened, Chip sacrificed much to be the second parent to us. He would be the one to stay at home and be available when we returned from school. He was there to make sure we were well-fed, clothed, there to help us with our homework, and there while my father traveled for days, weeks, sometimes for a month at a time.

But how brave of him to plunge head first, or perhaps I should say heart first, into the flying shrapnel of a dismantled family with a man ten years his senior and his two pre-pubescent children. While I was screaming in my head, "I want Daddy and only Daddy," Parker was wondering where Mommy was. Privately, I was wondering that, too, but I pretended she simply didn't exist. What a lot of baggage for Chip to take on. How brave indeed. The clincher is that Chip hung in there, with all of the rejections and disappointments. He never gave up on us or on me. So great was his love and his commitment. In the meantime, I provoked, upset, and ignored him, while I stopped dancing altogether for two years.

Which way?

As I pushed off and on from dancing, I was met with guilt attached to the possibility of not choosing the thing my parents had chosen. My father knew that I struggled with the subject of my dancing. But more than my brother and I following in his footsteps was his greater desire to see us happy with whatever we chose to do. It was at this point in our lives that Parker, with all his promise and focus, seemed the one destined for greatness.

My father's favorite nickname for him was Pip, from the novel *Great Expectations*. He always considered Parker to be a boy of great promise. As a dancer, he was the little boy with the beautiful feet, high jump, and effortless flexibility. He was also a natural and gifted athlete. In school he was strong in math, with a head for making and squirreling away money, while money burned a hole in my pocket. He made the honor roll consistently in elementary and high school, while I was often barely passing. If he'd had an interest towards that end, his street smarts, competitive nature and strategic mind could have made him an excellent attorney. He could even draw well. He possessed all of these attributes with good looks and charm to boot. It was all there for him, the possibilities and opportunities, to create a great life. We were all eager to see what he would do with it all.

But I remained in limbo, as I decided which fork in the road I would take.

Velvet Magazine

Meanwhile, my mother packed up, sold the brownstone on West Brookline Street (not a smart move), and moved to Los Angeles. By the time she moved to California, we had moved to Englewood, New Jersey, and I had entered public school.

Since separating herself from us, my mother seemed to lead a very secretive life. Getting an answer from her about what she was doing was a big challenge. Her responses were always vague and mysterious. We had no idea what her life was like in California. She wasn't teaching nor was she dancing anymore. She was dabbling in piano and singing, but how was she surviving once the alimony stopped coming?

My father tried to keep us in touch with her but she withdrew. The more she withdrew, the more I shut down a desire to speak with her. This mysterious life of the former revered ballerina, once sought after by the likes of George Balanchine and Maurice Bejart, would later blow our minds when the secret became revealed. A dear friend to both my parents during their Boston years felt it necessary and with good intent to pass on some disturbing news to my father.

When I was fifteen years old, my father decided that I was old enough to know from him, rather than from someone else, what in fact my mother had been doing. From one of his khaki-colored file cabinets, hidden behind clothes in his brown and beige comfy dressing room, he presented me with a magazine. He had a pained and heartbreaking look on his face. I read the cover: *Velvet Magazine*. I recall a lot of deep purples and splashes of red on a black background. He had dog-eared certain pages.

My mother had descended into the depths of erotic dancing and its underworld. There were several pages featuring her pole dancing in X-rated poses. More than that, I don't feel the necessity to elaborate. Let us just say it was a newly discovered reality I tried very hard to forget.

I look back on the years in Boston, during those hot summers and am reminded of my mother's blatant physical display. As I think about her need for attention and affirmation, Blanche Dubois from *A Streetcar Named Desire* comes to mind. When Parker and I were still preteens, she would send my father clippings of her headlining erotic shows; those clippings apparently were meant for our eyes as well. She wrote, "Don't forget to show this to the children. Love, Mommie."

Naturally my father kept it to himself. There was also a steady stream of tapes of her singing and playing piano that would make their way to our mailbox. It was always all about her and what she was doing. I believe her sense of reality had veered from its axis years before. She referred to us as her "little pumpkins" until we were well into our twenties. I perceived it more as a lack of awareness as opposed to a term of endearment.

As my dear friend Gabri once pointed out, maybe next to being a prima ballerina of a big ballet company, that was all my mother knew. She knew how to use her body, whether it was in an opera house or at a strip club. This was how she survived, but for me, especially at that age, it was shocking, embarrassing, and incredibly depressing.

I was ashamed to have her as a mother and ashamed to be her daughter. So ashamed, in fact, that as my body developed into that of a young woman, unless I had to show it off for an audition, I always covered up. I wore my father's big shirts to hide my full bosom and was afraid of tight-fitting clothes. As a teenager, I forced myself to wear tight things in order to fit in; if you had a body like mine, you were supposed to flaunt it. The attention my body got and the effect that it had made me afraid if it. As a budding performer, I showed it off, but in private I hid.

For many years, I didn't understand why I was so self-conscious, but I later came to the realization that I didn't want to be found out. Somehow, if I covered up, I wouldn't be discovered to be the daughter of a middle-aged former international ballerina who slid down greasy poles along the Sunset Strip. The efforts I made to hide my voluptuousness meant chances were good that I might not end up like her. I desperately did not want to be like her. I didn't want to be like her so much that to me she was dead.

It wasn't until I was much older that I ever talked about my mother. When anyone asked me about her, I simply wrote her off as crazy. Those closest to me knew not to bring up the subject of her or her absence. I became a very angry, cynical young lady. I was hopelessly sarcastic and sullen. I became hard on myself as well as others in an effort to do battle with all the forces I perceived to be out to get me. On the day I was introduced to *Velvet Magazine*, any glimmer of hope or possibility for loving my mother ceased. Our fate was sealed and I no longer cared to understand her. Or so I thought.

The real truth was that I did love her and therein lay the struggle for me. I was so hurt I didn't want to love. I hated myself for not hating her enough. Hated myself for still loving her. I didn't know all of this then. I might have fooled most people. Most of my friends and family believed I was coping. I always appeared cool, often chilly, in fact, and in control of my emotions. How absurd. How could I have been? How, at twelve, thirteen, and fifteen could I have been?

Tick tick

The discovery of the unforgettable news about my mother in some subconscious way unhinged my spirit more deeply about things, about people, and about myself. If, prior to that moment, I'd been drifting a bit in my decisions to wholly commit to some thing or other, following that discovery I became adrift with more purpose. It was a contradictory state of being and a potentially volatile combination. On the one hand, I became even more clear and driven with a fiercer momentum in following my dreams, while on the other hand I was emotionally more fragile than ever. I was left with some kind of feverish clock within me that was tick, tick, ticking. Feelings within me wound tighter, as I was desperately reaching to achieve something higher. As my insides became chaos, my mind led me with renewed clarity to that which enticed my shifting appetite.

Soon after leaving Dance Theatre of Harlem, I became interested in doing commercial work and acting. There are two things that almost everyone secretly wants: to be a movie star and to write a book. Lydia Abarca, one of the great ballet beauties formerly with DTH, put me in touch with a management company called Kids 'n Company. I read some copy for them and they liked me. This was the early '80s, and not everyone looked the way I did yet: the "mulatto" skin color and big corkscrew curls. Of course we were out there, but were not yet a tapped commodity.

The goal in the world of entertainment is to make everything work for you. I had an added advantage with my dancing background to potentially obtain more work, so I began taking classes again to stay in shape. I was leaving the more methodical and prescribed world of ballet behind for the smorgasbord of showbiz! The only difference was that when I wasn't taking class, auditioning or in school, I was partying. It was a decadent period, and I was growing up right in the heart of all its drug-induced color and splendor.

My friends and I were fourteen, fifteen, and sixteen years old, getting the other half of our education and worldly experience in the bathroom stalls of Xenon, Limelight and Studio 54. Although it was the tail end of "Studio," we got the best of what it still had to offer. We could still spot Andy Wharhol, Grace Jones, or Bianca Jagger hanging together in the VIP section of the club. While Sylvester sang "Do You Wanna Funk?" into the morning hours, we had a smashing good time pretending to be grown up, careless, and smug. My dear heart, Anthony Barrile, dubbed us *The Peanuts Gang* because we led very independent lives at very young ages. He described all of our parents as being in the background, shown only from the waist down, speaking in *wah wah wah* language like Charlie Brown's Miss Othmar.

We all got thoroughly wasted often thanks to a cornucopia of the best heady appetizers. There were bong hits, roaches, hash brownies, Quaaludes, bennies, and any liquor combination imaginable, but the favorite of that time, of course, was cocaine. Many did heroin, but I didn't go there. And we girls rarely paid for anything and never paid to get into clubs. It was all about the "guest list" and knowing the bouncers. We would leave a club before deigning to pay. We were a part of the New York City brat pack. We were a multi-culti *St. Elmo's Fire live,* which also included from time to time Robert Downey Jr. and Sarah Jessica Parker. It was truly an incredible and wickedly fun time. Crazy fun, crazy wild, and sometimes crazy dangerous.

Without a doubt, there were situations I was lucky to have walked away from unharmed. We were a fortunate group. However, even while sitting on the floor hunched over a glass table snorting from hundred dollar bills and silver spoons in the company of Playboy Playmates and drug dealers who stashed guns under beds and stuffed rolls of cash in the freezer, I knew that I was in the middle of a phase.

Thankfully, I wasn't born with an addictive personality and heard frequently from a little voice that whispered persuasively in my ear when enough was enough. And lucky for me, I listened. Early on during this bacchanalian period, I made a pact with myself that no matter where I'd been or what I'd done the night before, I would always call to let my father know that I was all right. Many times I'd be walking out of a club at the crack of dawn, dressed in next to nothing on the way to the Empire Diner or some other early morning breakfast haunt to deal with my interminable munchies. Still, I'd slip into a phone booth or wake up at a friend's place to make my call home. Sometimes, the day after a long night I'd need to pull it together for an audition or a job, but I was never too messed up to keep me from being professional. I never wanted to jeopardize my work or my opportunities.

Then one night there came a point when I'd gotten a little too high and I'd crashed a little too hard. I ended it that night and haven't had a sniff or a pop or a bong hit since. Unfortunately, a lot of lost souls got swept away during that time. They rode the white horse of heroin to their young graves and they also served as a reminder of how I categorically did *not* want to end up. I'm grateful I let that phase pass me by.

∽⊙∾

"Can I offer you a cold beverage? A Pepsi product, glass of wine, or a Bloody Mary?" The flight attendant clearly has an ear on my reverie but she obviously didn't catch the end of my story. The sky outside of the airplane window is pitch black. I'm suddenly aware of snoring around me.

"No, thank you, I think I'll pass. Water would be great." She smiles with practiced approval and after a sip of water I disappear once again from the here and now, opting instead for the momentary return to my past.

∽᷊᷈᷉∾

Film crazy

Almost everyone I know has a secret place of longing. It's not so much a regret as a hidden curiosity to fulfill a deeper dream. It's something like: *If I could do anything...* or *I've always wanted to...* My father was unquestionably and before everything else, a dancer. Nonetheless, he secretly always wanted to be in the movies. He grew up living for the next picture show. At that time, in the 1940's, attending a picture show was quite an occasion. One got dressed up because the event was special, especially after a week of trying to scrape together the .25¢admission. Live music and cartoons preceded the major motion picture. It was at those Philadelphia movie houses that little black children like Billy Wilson could imagine and dream about a life of glamour and dramatic excitement. Hollywood had him rapt: hook, line and sinker. It was all there, up on the silver screen: beauty, romance, style, intrigue, humor, and larger-than-life characters.

It was also through the movies—while watching *The Red Shoes*—that his love for the ballet world was born. In the movies anything was possible. That idea, coupled with the reinforcement from his parents and with the support of their caring black community, made him sure he was to become a star that would one day shine brightly. Although Fred and Ginger strongly influenced his direction toward a more commercial style, he also found a kinship with the actors and the brilliance of the spoken word.

He greatly respected the fine actors and great stars of that era—Garbo, Dietrich, Orson Welles, Hepburn and Tracy, Gregory Peck, Olivier, Vivian Leigh, Jason Robards, and, of course, Bette Davis. His great love affair with movies encompassed every aspect. His eye went to every nuance of creating the great films. It was the lighting, make-up, clothes; the directing, staging, camera angles; the gesture, action, and stillness. It was a world in which he could submerge, which was different from how he dived into creating a ballet or mounting a show. It was his unfulfilled passion.

Early in my childhood he passed on his adoration of film to me, and I embraced it with the same giddy pleasure. Watching movies was one of our favorite ways to spend a day or a weekend together. It was also a terrific education for me. He knew the name of every actor, cameo or lead; writer; director;, and choreographer; and often the dramas behind the drama. Watching movies together was the only time we could exercise the freedom of verbal commentary without being reprimanded. We could have ongoing conversations while still enjoying the film. This made anyone else completely crazy. Whatever we missed we rewound, fast-forwarded or paused. We had our own groove and we loved it. We didn't discriminate; a really bad film could be a lot of fun, too.

He loved a great love story as well as a good action film. If he had to choose, it probably would have been a great thriller or some inventive story with a macabre or perverse twist. He adored "clever" and frightening: intelligent, erotic, sensual, stylish and always … entertaining. Some of his favorite films were *Great Expectations; The Little Foxes; Now, Voyager; Midnight Cowboy; The Godfather; Last Tango in Paris; The Deer Hunter; I'm Dancing as Fast as I Can; The Way We Were; Midnight Express; Jaws; The Exorcist; Body Double; Dressed to Kill; Close Encounters of the Third Kind; Maurice*; and, of course, *Mommie Dearest*, among many, many others.

All of us grew up with the ritual of movie going. It is also a typically New York pastime. On Sundays you put on your favorite baseball cap, you get your cup o' joe, your bagel, your Sunday *Times* and figure out what movie you're gonna see.

My father had found in Chip a part-time partner in crime with movie going, but Chip couldn't go two rounds with a movie at home. We'd put the second film on and Chip would usually succumb to a nap. My father sat in his favorite wing chair and I was usually stretched out or balled up on the sofa, the two of us being on a movie mission as we pressed on into the night. The weekends at our house in Jersey were movie marathon days.

But before the marathon, one of his biggest treats to himself was getting his car washed. It was a running joke, however true, that whenever he had the car washed it would rain. Regardless, he was always so excited about this ritual. "Come on Chip! Holly, Parker, come with me to get the car washed."

We would jump. It was one of those reliable simple events we all enjoyed. We enjoyed it mostly because we were with him. It is one of my fondest recollections. It is evidence of the least glamorous, least material, least expensive joys of being a family. The car wash was usually followed by picking up fresh flowers for the house and maybe a few red, ripe Jersey tomatoes. It was the makings of a perfect Wilson weekend.

We'd rent two to six films. Next we'd make sure we had all the necessary edibles or "eats." Very important. It was difficult for him to watch a movie without his salty potato chips, sour pickles and ginger ale. We'd make ourselves a delicious sandwich of tuna with apples or a BLT with our chips and ice-cold ginger ales, get organized with pillows and afghans close at hand and sink into the cinema. Those were glorious times that we shared and relished. It was those cozy and familiar weekend den memories with Dad that replaced the sadness I lived with at not having my mother in my life.

Chip would join us during the drama or comedy, but we'd usually lose him with a foreign film or something scary and graphic. Parker would join us for the scary, graphic, and action films, but we'd lose him during the romance. Sometimes we'd lose him to the endless series of beeps coming from his hyperactive beeper. Parker could not sit still for very long anyway. His tempo was of someone who needs to be somewhere else—always on the go. My brother and his friends might float in or out, but Dad and I would sit there until we'd run our movie magic to the end. It seemed that with each film, we could extract some new piece of a thing that helped us to understand this world and ourselves a bit better. I was also realizing more and more that I, too, had a craving to be a part of that world and not only as spectator.

Daddy's little girl in Positano, Italy. (1967) Alexis Wilson collection.

dance and dancers

October 1962 2s 6d/Festivals — Amsterdam, Edinburgh, Stockholm/Marceau talks/India Dances /The Ballet That Never Was

◄ LE PALAIS DE CRISTAL:
Sonja van Beers and Billy Wilson
in Leone de Mail's reconstruction
of the work which Balanchine
originally created to Bizet's symphony

North Circular 4

CLIVE BARNES at the Holland Festival in Amsterdam sees
The Netherlands National Ballet in a programme of
four works

WHY IS IT, I WONDER, THAT SOME OF THE MOST BALLET-CONSCIOUS of communities have to struggle the hardest to form a national ballet? The instance I am thinking of is Holland, but I might just as easily have selected Australia. There seems to be an intense interest in Holland in all forms of theatrical dancing, but the history of its national ballet is a strange and, to the outsider, a labarynthine affair.

My invaluable *Dance Encyclopaedia* assures me that: 'Until 1934 no dance tradition existed in Holland,' and indeed it seems that *classical* ballet did not take root until after the war. The Dutch public pre-war was apparently exclusively interested in the Central European and modern dance. The first moves towards a national group was taken in 1936 by the German choreographer Yvonne Georgi.

When during the war-time occupation a Dutch opera was founded in Amsterdam in 1941, the Georgi group was engaged as an opera ballet. Georgi, herself a one-time pupil of Jooss, was not a classical choreographer, although as the interest in classical ballet mounted during the war, she took the opportunity to include a certain amount of classical technique in her modern dance choreography. After the war Georgi returned to Germany, and the opera and ballet were closed down for a time by the Dutch authorities. In July 1946 the Amsterdam Opera was re-organised and a small ballet group was attached to it. As the activities of some of the dancers who had worked there during the war were not acceptable to the liberated Government, such dancers were not allowed to work in the post-war ballet. For a time the prospects of ballet in Holland looked very bleak indeed.

However, quite soon companies in Holland proliferated. A few years ago the main companies were the Nederlands Ballet, directed by Sonia Gaskell, the Ballet der Lage Landen, directed by Mascha ter Weeme, the Amsterdam Opera Ballet, directed by Françoise Adret, and the Scapino Ballet, a company primarily for children. A series of successful takeover bids clarified the situation. The Ballet der Lage Landen and the Amsterdam Opera Ballet were originally fused under the direction of Mascha ter Weeme, and this season that company was itself fused with the Nederlands Ballet, and is now known as Het Nationale Ballet, under the main direction of Sonia Gaskell, although its opera activities remain the responsibility of Mascha ter Weeme. Although this is of course the principal company, the Scapino Ballet is continuing its valuable work with children, and a third company, the Neder-

lands Dans Teater, has been formed under the direction of American ballet-master and choreographer Benjamin Harkavy.

The repertory of this new National Ballet has been taken from the Gaskell group, thus several of the more significant creations of the Ballet der Lage Landen — such as Jack Carter's *The Witch Boy*, which was originally created for this company — appear to have been dropped, at least temporarily. The new repertory is enormous. It lists no less than fifty-six ballets, with its choreographers including Fokine, Balanchine, Massine, Lichine, Skibine, Lifar, Petit, Lander, Taras, Herbert Ross, Jack Carter, Pearl Lang, a number of Dutch choreographers, Marius Petipa, Vincenzo Galeotti and, not improbably, Uncle Tom Cobbley. To dance this formidable repertory the company has a roster of seventy-nine dancers; made up of eighteen principals, fourteen senior soloists, eleven junior soloists, thirteen senior *corps de ballet* and twenty-three junior *corps de ballet*. There are three ballet-masters attached to the company, Karel Shook, Margot van Wilgenburg and Roland Casenave, and two resident choreographers, Rudi van Dantzig and Robert Kaesen. Although I was unable to find out precisely how much money it got from the Dutch Government, I understand that it is very adequately subsidised.

The Netherlands National Ballet is a more than welcome addition to the European dance scene. It is one of the largest of the national ballets — larger for example than the Royal Danish Ballet, or any German company or, indeed, than the Covent Garden section of the Royal Ballet. Its modern repertory is unequalled in its scope and ambition. If any repertory had the right to be regarded as ballet's Museum of Modern Art, this is it. The only omissions to be found are representative works by British choreographers (although British ballet has never been particularly successful with the surprisingly powerful Dutch critics) and Jerome Robbins.

As everyone must agree, it takes a long time to form a national ballet, and there is no doubt that like Thursday's Child the Netherlands National Ballet has far to go. On the other hand, it is very pleasant to find that Holland nowadays has a ballet company which it can put up at its own finely varied Holland Festival, and let it stand on its own seventy-nine pairs of feet amid the multifarious international attractions.

The Holland Festival is unique in covering a country rather than an individual town, and this year the Netherlands Ballet gave two performances in Amsterdam, one in Arnhem, one

My mother and father (Sonja van Beers & Billy Wilson) dancing together "Le Palais De Cristal" originally created by Balanchine to Bizet's symphony. (1962) Alexis Wilson collection.

Dad causing a commotion in Barcelona, Spain. Alexis Wilson collection.

Taken by Dad's longtime friend Alvin Ailey. Alexis Wilson collection.

In London. Photo taken by ©Robert Belton. Alexis Wilson collection.

Rehearsing 'Othello' with choreographer Serge Lifar (1959). Photo taken by ©Maria Austria. Alexis Wilson collection.

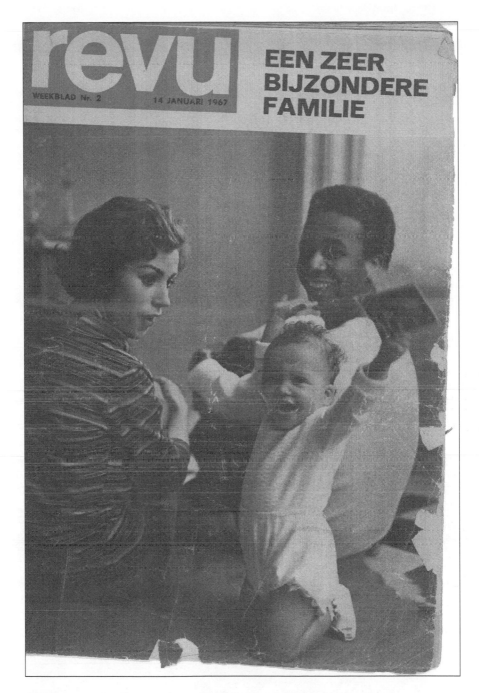

My father, my mother and me on the cover of REVU Magazine in Amsterdam, Holland. (1967). Photo taken by ©Maria Austria. Alexis Wilson collection.

Performing in Boston circa '74. Photo taken by ©John Lindquist. Alexis Wilson collection.

With my mother on Paradise Island in The Bahamas. Alexis Wilson collection.

Little me standing at the barre at 7 years old. Photo taken by Everett R. Profit. Alexis Wilson collection.

My favorite black & white photo of my father, my brother & me, taken by The New York Times. Photo courtesy of ©Christopher Little. Alexis Wilson Collection.

My first professional dance photo taken by ©Daniel Lee. NYC (1976). Alexis Wilson collection.

Me dancing Peasant pas de Deux (The Dance Theatre of Harlem Open House). At age fourteen with Edgar Richards (1979). Photo courtesy of ©Jack Vartoogian/FrontRowPhotos.

The beautiful and talented Chip Garnett. Alexis Wilson collection.

Press photo for BUBBLING BROWN SUGAR (Dad, Vivian Reed & Avon Long). Alexis Wilson collection.

The Dutch paper, De Telegraaf, did a story on my father and me when I joined the cast of his show A NIGHT AT THE COTTON CLUB. (1989) Photo courtesy of ©Henk van der Meyden. Alexis Wilson collection.

Alexis Wilson

The last 8X10 that I used for auditions in the 90's. Photo taken by ©Nick Granito in NYC. Alexis Wilson collection.

Dancing the tango with John Fredo in HARLEM SUITE, directed and choreographed by Maurice Hines. Photo taken by Bert Andrews. (1988). Alexis Wilson collection.

In D.C. after a performance of HARLEM SUITE. Todd Hunter, Maurice Hines, Chip, Dad, and me (1988). Alexis Wilson collection.

*Alvin Ailey American Dance Theater Gala and premier of WINTER IN
LISBON (with David Campbell and my father). Chip was supposed to
attend with my father but he was admitted into St. Vincent's. Alexis Wilson
collection.*

Opening night of the musical JOSEPHINE in Amsterdam with my father. One of the last photos taken of us while he was still healthy. Alexis Wilson collection.

CHAPTER 9

GROWING PAINS AND GROWING UP

AUDITIONED FOR ANYTHING that came my way, and I booked a lot of commercials that led to being seen for film and the occasional TV project. Movies have always held the greatest fascination for me, and I wanted that the most. At the time, I was auditioning over and over for the speaking part of the sister to Gregory and Maurice Hines in a movie developing a lot of buzz: *The Cotton Club*, to be directed by Frances Ford Coppola and starring Richard Gere and Diane Lane. There was a parallel story line that served as a peek into life behind the Cotton Club. That sub-plot featured Gregory and Maurice—brothers on and off the screen—along with Lonette McGee as Gregory's love interest. The role that I wanted had come down to a few of us, including talk of Whitney Houston and Irene Cara. When a friend of mine, Wynnona Smith, landed the part, I was hired on the spot by choreographer George Faison to dance in the movie.

The Cotton Club was one of those rare projects. There was constant drama surrounding it. The making of it could have been a film in and of itself. It was unique in that an abundance of black artists of talent and beauty were sifted out and brought on board. Although it was the '80s, this kind of thing still didn't happen very often, making for a novel and thrilling experience.

Every gorgeous black male and female model I'd ever seen or at one time had up on my wall had been hired, from Tracey Ross to Mario Van Peebles.

All of the divas and all of the gypsies—the dancers who go from show to show—were there. The best hoofers were collected, the best dancers assembled, singers and "lookers" were gathered. It was a feast of beauty and talent, including the most exciting up-and-coming young black actors, such as Laurence Fishburne and Giancarlo Esposito. Along with the talent was a laundry list of choreographers and creative people who were famously hired and fired. Perhaps the only choreographer not hired had been my father. He and Gregory Hines did not play at being bosom buddies. My father was not much of a kowtower and some past negative history between them on *Eubie!* was never resolved.

Contrary to what many black artists believed, *The Cotton Club* was not a film about the Cotton Club, but a gangster movie with black entertainment as its backdrop. The glamour and excitement of the brazenly segregated showbiz of that era served to support the bloody drama and the love story. The film boasted a stunning cast led by a master: Mr. Coppola. It was an opportunity that I fully soaked up and basked in. It was during that project I became great friends with Maurice Hines. At the set location in Astoria, Queens, I hung out primarily on the hair and make-up floor with the actors. Wynnona and I became even closer friends, and our buddies were Giancarlo, Laurence, Maurice, Ed O'Ross, and "Ziggy." I was a fly on the wall. Laurence and Giancarlo were like renegades on the set, spreading the word of the real political scene that was at work. They talked about creative injustice. They wanted the storyline to emphasize the Cotton Club story and not just be the brown-sugar, pretty backdrop to a gangster/love story. I melted in their presence. But they could have been talking about anything. I just wanted to be around them, around their talent and their charisma.

Most of the cast heard what they were saying, but to be frank, folks were just happy to have a gig and do it with some old friends. That's often the way it is. No creative coup was about to happen on the set of that movie, and everyone had the utmost respect for the director at the helm. It was also a pretty extravagant movie for that time. The budget seemed limitless, with a seemingly endless need for still more funds. Everyone used cab vouchers, for everything from getting to and from the set to a little shopping. But Laurence and Giancarlo tried to keep our awareness up. It was a priceless experience. I'd spent my whole growing up glued to watching movies with my father, but it was during the filming of *The Cotton Club* that I truly became hooked on film and acting.

Learning the craft

I was coming close to getting many parts I was up for, but I wasn't landing them. This pattern culminated with the great disappointment of my not getting the role of Squeak in the film *The Color Purple*, a role I wanted so badly and the book of which I'd read inside-out and upside-down. The monologue I did on tape for that audition was terrible. It was a tough scene in the life of this character, and I had no idea how to bring that to the table. I knew nothing about how to call on unfamiliar emotions in that way. After that letdown, I was resolved to study the craft.

Clearly, I could no longer depend on my intuition to get me a real acting job. In commercials it had worked for me, but for film I would need much more. I had worked on *The Cotton Club* during my senior high school year at Dwight Morrow High School in New Jersey. I ended up spending some of that filming time living with Sarah Jessica Parker, with whom I'd attended both PCS and Dwight Morrow, while she filmed *Footloose* with Herbert Ross, an old friend of my father's. After filming was done and I'd graduated from high school, I took a year off, with no intention of going to college. However, my father insisted I go back to school and encouraged me to leave New York to take advantage of a different kind of experience.

By the following year, I knew where I wanted to go and it was the only school I applied to. My father had been an artist-in-residence at Carnegie Mellon University for a year or more before I became interested. Mel Shapiro, who had worked with my father on *Stop the World – I Want to Get Off*, brought him there. Dad would return home from C.M.U so excited by what was going on: the talent, the study, and especially what Mel was doing with the department. He kept saying, "Holly, you've got to come and visit this school." As usual, I relented and I did visit. I walked into the College of Fine Arts building, with its marble floors, the sweet cacophony of rehearsal room instruments with notes bouncing off the deep wood doors, and I fell in love. That was where I wanted to be. My father was right again.

C.M.U. was like being in the best kind of therapy for four years straight. It was challenging because, as an actor, the process forces you to reveal so much of yourself. It was an incredible journey both invigorating and competitive. Those were elements I was already used to but in a completely different environment. Each semester we stood a chance of being "cut" from the program. By our senior year, we had less than half of our original class intact. I continued to audition for things when back in New York during school breaks or to fly in and out if I had the opportunity to be seen for something important. Consequently, I did some short-term work at times throughout the school year whenever possible. It didn't happen all the time, but when it did, I took advantage. The plus was having my father at the school off and on throughout the year to help guide me. If I wasn't taking his required dance class, I was in rehearsal for one of the many main stage productions he did for the Pittsburgh paying public.

Sometimes, being my father's daughter brought undue angst and stress, while at the same time providing me with an instant entrée to people in the business. However, it took many years before I graciously took advantage of the groundwork he'd laid for both my brother and me. I needed to prove myself on my terms and gain my own credibility, not because I was Billy Wilson's daughter. Ah, those idyllic stubborn and rebellious college years. Gradually, the older I became, the more I celebrated and embraced the blessings that came along with my father's hard work and accomplishments. He would have wanted it no other way. He'd say, "You want to work? I'm doing a show. Take the job!" What a gift. If it's there for you, grab it! My four years at C.M.U were indispensible. I was slowly becoming my own person, complete with my own desires and aspirations. I also had a lot of worries about my young non-existent love life.

Hard talk

As I look back on all the many phases of my life growing up with my father, I am reminded that regardless of any disagreements we had over the years, he was right there to gently guide and support me. I was not an easy adolescent, but he had steadfast faith in who I was at my core. He essentially trusted my basic judgment. His trust and belief in me gave me great courage and comfort. I recall one particularly poignant moment between us that has always stayed with me. It was a rite of passage he seemed to be taking right along with me.

I was getting ready to go back to college after one of my school breaks, packing by bags in my rose-colored bedroom with the rarely used small fireplace surrounded by white stucco. It was late in the afternoon, just before sunset. My door was wide open and bright lights were on throughout the upstairs. Everyone was busy doing his own thing. This was the house on Robin Road in Englewood, my favorite house in New Jersey. I was crying and it was becoming uncontrollable. My father came in and stood in the doorway looking at me and my wet face. In my head I was saying: *Please don't ask. Please don't ask me.*

"What's wrong with you, Holly, that you're crying like this?" he asked and that question sent me wailing into more tears. It came pouring and tumbling out of me. I couldn't tell him and wasn't even able to try in between my sobs.

"Well, something must be wrong. Tell me." He sat on the edge of my bed. "What *is* it Holly?" I remember pacing back and forth, carrying clothes absentmindedly to my bag. *Keep moving, keep moving, keep moving!* He patted the bed softly for me to sit next to him. I sat, trying to calm down and find the safe break in between my crying to say what I didn't know I'd been feeling. Feeling for some years, I suppose. My door remained wide open, but apparently Parker and Chip knew to keep on their own course and not wander even a few feet in the direction of what was going on in my room. We had this emotional moment to ourselves.

After a few long and pregnant pauses, "I'm just ... afraid that I'll never find any ... one." Again came the tidal waves of inconsolable tears.

"That you'll never find anyone?"

"That I'll always be alone."

"Why would you think that, Holly?"

"Because ..."

"Because why?"

"I've never had a boyfriend."

"Oh, Holly."

"No, it's true!"

"You've had boys you were interested in."

"Yes, but I've never brought them home."

"Why not?" Then came another tremendous and scary pause. He had asked.

"I could never bring them home." He let me go on. I think for the first time he considered what I might say and was probably more afraid than I was at my reply.

"I don't bring anyone home because I don't want to explain. You and Chip." There, I had said it. I was at once relieved and filled like a balloon with sorry guilt.

"Oh, Holly. I never knew that. I never even thought that might be a reason for ..." I remember his eyes welling up. I felt so sorry.

"But you know, you *will* find someone. I promise you that." And the tears began rolling down his face. I was stunned. Everything around me stopped. I was simply quiet. I waited. I listened. "You know, I had this same conversation with your godfather years ago when I was about your age. I was feeling very alone and sometimes like I was the only one on the planet in my feelings about so many things. I would put on sad records and sit alone getting very melancholy. Karel reassured me. He told me I would fall in love over and over again. He was right. And one day, *you* will find someone truly wonderful." We both sat there, and I loved him more than ever.

"I'm so sorry you've felt that way about Chip and me. I would always hope you would feel good enough about yourself and your family that you could bring anyone home. But I can't apologize for my life with Chip. That's just what it is. And he loves you two so much. He would feel awful knowing that you felt this way. This is your home and you must always feel comfortable to come here. We love you. But don't worry about being alone. You're too young to be worrying about that. You're gonna have so many men in your life, I'm gonna have to beat them away with a stick." We hugged and I wanted to stay wrapped in those safe and protecting arms forever.

As much as the memory of that difficult moment between my father and me brings back some of the sadness, its importance lay in my father's caring and beautiful honesty. I loved him not only for telling me what I very much needed to hear, but also for sharing a bit more of himself with me. He was reminding me that he too was young once and had felt all the ups and downs of growing pains. I think of all the chaperoning, the financial bailouts and handouts to support all the many fads and phases, the sneaky stories during the club days, the countless honest conversations, the "but I need that jacket!" moments, the calls from Mommy once a year that would consistently disrupt and disturb our very nice day. There were the tiny diamonds of advice before the important auditions and the bond of love among our family of four when things got tough.

✎

As I recline the airplane seat back to fall deeper, my mind is swirling with memories that are difficult to keep up with. They sit like delicate black and white snapshots in growing numbers, shuffling like cards and peeling off from sturdy shelves throughout my mind. I think of Karel's passing.

✎

Chi-Chi died of cancer on July 25, 1985. We all attended his funeral, only the second one that Parker and I had experienced, and I remember its being very strange. Although I was no longer a child by that time, I recall the day feeling very surreal. All of these people milling around. People I knew and people I didn't know. And in the heavy-looking box lay my godfather. I knew that Karel's physical being was in that box, but I also knew that his spirit was on the outside floating all around us.

He was the kind of man and artist who lived for the things he was passionate about. It didn't matter that he walked out onto the street with the dance shoes he'd worn all day teaching and rehearsing in. Money didn't seem to mean all that much to him, although I'm sure it did. Later in his life, all he wanted to buy was a Subaru. In all those years, I'd never known him to carry another shoulder bag, possess more than two jackets or wear a hat to cover that gorgeous head of silver hair, even in the dead of winter. Things that concerned the average person just seemed to swirl around him, unnoticed. If he had dancers to teach, his cigarettes waiting for him crushed in his jacket pocket, good food, drink, and people around to share it with, I believe he was happy. I know he worried about Max, his black Manx cat. I do know that for all that contentment something did ring *unfulfilled*.

Before my godfather had become ill, my father commented that Karel was slowly committing suicide by ignoring the advice of friends and doctors telling him he must quit smoking. Even when his larynx was removed, he was determined to continue to smoke and drink himself, quite literally, to death. When he was ill, I couldn't seem to get past my own fears enough to visit him. Parker, however, would visit him every day after school. After the operation, he spoke with a kind of microphone-looking white device pressed against the gauze of his throat. It scared me. He would press a cigarette against the gauzed up hole and inhale to keep getting his fix. It was too bizarre and shocking for me to watch.

Parker seemed somehow able to laugh and have fun with him as usual. I learned a lot from Parker at that time. Though he was only eleven or twelve, he was so much stronger than I could be then. I ran away from what I thought might be inevitable and lost out on all of the last possible precious moments I could have spent with my only wonderful godfather. Had I been around as things wound down for him, he could have made me laugh a little more or perhaps more importantly, I could have made *him* laugh. He could have shared some impossible recipes with me, passed on words of wisdom, and whispered nearly inaudible stories that only we would have known about. That would have been even more delicious than his rack of lamb.

I never got a chance to talk about Karel's history with my father, but there was sorrow there and a bitter taste at not having felt fully appreciated. And who were *his* great loves? Had they all moved on to find other things and other people? I have vivid and festive memories of the summer months in his house when he always had an old friend or younger male dancer staying with him, but we never knew or heard of anyone seriously in his life. Regardless of that, he had affected people's and artists' lives immeasurably and profoundly. He had been great in his life and made an unforgettable and important impact on my brother and me.

Karel adored the two of us. Not one more than the other but in huge, unabashed, loving equal doses. He loved us without self-consciousness or apology. He spoiled us shamefully and would have done anything for us, as I believe he had for our father as well. He unknowingly helped me to learn how to love in difficult times, when loved ones need it most. Unfortunately, I was unable to rise to this occasion during his time of need, but in hindsight I took from his death a vow never to bow out when things get uncomfortable or tough and never to abandon anyone else I love again. It was the thing, the event, to inspire and steel me for what was to come with friends, with Chip, and especially with my father.

I miss Chi-Chi. I miss his never missing the opportunity to slip me some change when I was a little girl or make me laugh or push me harder. He was a divine and original spirit. We've all missed him terribly, but I like to imagine a place where he, Chip, and my father have fresh tumblers of whatever they wish, with cigarettes between their long fingers—the way they all did in a more carefree time—while laughing and cooking and feeling like kings.

On tour

After my first year at Carnegie Mellon, I switched from a musical theater major to straight acting. I had little use for the frivolity of musical theater and opted for the "serious" stuff instead. Being a straight actor was regarded as the more substantial and more worthy craft of the two. In those days, musical theater and soap operas were still looked down upon. Musical theater students were loud, animated and silly. I wanted to be taken seriously. Only later did I come back around to appreciate the complexities and multi-dynamics that must all come together to pull off a "silly" and "frivolous" musical. As the daughter of a musical theater choreographer, I should have known better—and someone should have put a bar of soap in my mouth.

I wanted to be seen as an actor first, then as a dancer. I don't know how it is today, but then it was not so easy to accomplish. When casting agents looked at my résumé, my pretty face and dancer's long body were all they saw. The reality was that I had more opportunities to continue to get work as an African American dancer than as an African American actress, as opposed to simply a dancer or an actor. Lest we forget, this was the period when a small explosion of black talent on TV and film was just *beginning* to take a new turn. *The Cosby Show* was on and *A Different World* had just come out of the wings. So when work came, even during my college years, as a dancer, I took it, whether it was a commercial or a musical. I was gradually learning how foolish it was to discriminate and I always loved making my own money. So when Maurice Hines called me at school to say he was creating a tango for me, as a feature, in his upcoming musical *Harlem Suite*, I accepted.

The show would star Jennifer Holiday and later Stephanie Mills, together with Maurice, who would also direct and choreograph. He'd called me the year before to offer me the role of Daisy in *Satchmo*, the life of Louis Armstrong. I had turned that down, as I was studying to become a serious actress. How ridiculous. I quickly learned that I would never hope to survive if I chose my work that way. My father probably wanted to shake me, but I have a feeling he respected my seriousness. *Satchmo* starred Byron Stripling, the heavy-hitting trumpet virtuoso who would later become my husband. By the time Maurice's second offer came around, I had actually been doing more and more musicals at school and was ready for something outside of C.M.U.

I was excited and looking forward to the adventure of being on tour. The commercial world would be much different than the ballet world. My father was thrilled and thought it would be a piece of cake for me. I was not so sure. I had only recently begun to turn my feet in and get a feeling for jazz. This was all fairly new to me, not to mention eight shows a week. I knew this would be a hard-dancing show but welcomed the challenge. Maurice was happy to have me and wanted me to come to D.C. early to be part of his "skeleton crew." The skeleton crew is made up of a select few dancers who serve as the skeleton for the choreographic work of a show, giving the choreographer an opportunity to work out some of the kinks of his ideas and create a basic structure before bringing the entire cast in. Not all choreographers work this way, but it can help to get a lot of work done and save some thinking time. There were about six of us. We would learn the choreography for roughly all the numbers in the show. With us he could create, throw away, shift, experiment and "set" the work. I was honored though terrified. Now I just had to get clearance from C.M.U. to leave during my final year because my taking the job would keep me out of school for four months or more.

I got the okay from the department head at the time, Elizabeth Orion, Mel Shapiro having left by my junior year. I was required to keep a detailed daily journal of my experience "on the road." I would in turn, receive full credit for my absence. I was, after all, doing the very thing I was studying to do. Blair Underwood had been my example. He was a new young talent who'd had a special place in my father's heart when he'd attended C.M.U a couple years before me. My father knew he was a star the moment he flashed that million-dollar smile. He'd left school to star on *L.A. Law* and never looked back. I was secretly hoping the same thing might happen to me.

Another reason for taking this gig was because I had had an increasing need to be surrounded by more people of color. I hadn't fallen in with the clique of black students outside of the drama department nor with the few of us within the department except for Charlie Johnson and Michael McElroy. Michael was one of my first friends at C.M.U. He has since gone on to do great work, starring in several productions on Broadway. I felt that not being a strong singer separated me from the black musical theater majors at C.M.U. They were all very strong vocally, especially the females. This was no one's fault other than my own. Despite Michael's constant encouragement for me to sing more, it was the thing I was the least confidant about.

Self-conscious or not, I would have to put my inferiority complex aside to do what was required of me in *Harlem Suite*. The other thing I would have to do was tap. I had tapped a bit. I learned a little from my father. I knew the tap finale from my father's show *Bubbling Brown Sugar* and had to tap a little in *The Cotton Club,* but you had to *tap* for Maurice Hines! There was no way around that. I had plenty of challenges ahead of me. It would not be a piece of cake. It would be more like a challenging, though heavenly rich, tiramisu.

The *Harlem Suite* experience would help to break me and force me to another level as a dancer and as a professional. And I did need to work on my tap, just like everyone else. The taps had to be clean. He demanded that. Fortunately, I was able to pick it up without too much problem, and where I was shaky I put myself in a corner and did it until I had it down. One thing I've never been unclear about is the absolute necessity to be a completely prepared professional in the goal to *deliver*. There were times when I got a little lost and nervous along the way—even made a few people crazy—but I always found my way back to where I needed to be. Being a bit of a perfectionist, I would pull and beg other dancers, on their breaks, no less, to go over a combination one more time with me. Maurice laughed at me. He knew I was working hard, but he never let me slide.

When we were in performance, the first two people at the theater each night were he and I. He would be listening to his Johnny Mathis, and I would simply soak up all I could. It was to be a defining period for me. Fast-forward to some months later, the show was a big success with full audiences but not enough money to keep it afloat. It did, however, run for close to six months, ending in L.A., but without me by that time.

Watching Jennifer Holiday from the wings each performance was a spectacular thrill and when Stephanie Mills took over the role, she was equally delicious in making it her own. I had the opportunity to work with some of the best dancers at that time such as Shaun Baker and Todd Hunter. Todd has remained one of my dearest friends and what a dancer! What a beauty, inside and out.

I also had the pleasure of witnessing the giant steps Maurice was taking as he was filling his own shoes as a respected choreographer. My father was always willing and wanting to give Maurice support and even the occasional advice when he sought it. With its exuberant performing style and high-octane energy, his choreography was finding its way to the next level and earning him big stripes in the business. I was proud to have been a part of that production. I had made new lifelong friends, forged a deeper friendship with Maurice, and laughed way too much. Although he ruined my knees with that damned tango, I'd do it all over again. By the end of the first leg of that tour, I was ready to return to C.M.U. and graduate with my class. The company took a break before going to California, and I went back to the sulfur smells of Pittsburgh.

That final year at Carnegie Mellon was my most challenging. I felt I was just beginning to work below my surface. Personally, although I'd never had a boyfriend to speak of, I did continue an off-and-on, highly charged relationship with an Italian someone of whom my father categorically did not approve, but who I naturally could not stay away from. We have remained friends to this day. Prior to meeting Byron, there have been three men in my life who will be forever dear. One brings to mind crazy days, the other makes me think of dancing amid windmills, and the third transports me to a downpour of rainy moments.

That final year created many memorable moments as well, and one of those moments found me soon after my return to school.

Gone wrong

One morning before the sun rose, my brother called from a hospital, and the news was with disturbing.

"Dad's car is totaled."

"What?"

"The car is totaled, Holly. I got into an accident."

"Oh, my God, Parker."

"I know."

"Are you all right?" I was then fully awake.

"Yeah, I'm okay. It was five cars."

"Wait a minute."

"I fell asleep at the wheel. The other cars were parked."

"Oh, my God."

"The paramedics said I shouldn't have walked way."

"What do you mean?"

"They couldn't believe it when they saw the car... You can't even tell what the car *looked* like. The accident was so bad I shoulda been killed, no joke."

"Are you sure you're okay?"

"Yeah, just some bruises and ..."

"No one else was hurt?"

"Nah." Pause. "Holly, you gotta call Dad."

"*I* gotta call?" I realized I'd heard his voice quivering. He was shaken and scared. "Okay, okay. Shit. I'm glad you're all right."

"Yeah, I know. Shit is crazy."

I did make the overseas call to Amsterdam where Chip and our father were working, to report what had happened and assure them that Parker was all right. I also told him the car was a memory. I have no idea what the total damage ended up being for my father, but later I did see the Polaroid of the little Toyota Celica—the first and last small car my father bought—and it looked like someone had crushed a tin can. The paramedics were right. Parker was a walking miracle. There had been other less traumatic events that he'd been involved in, but Parker's unscathed experience of that incident had proven to me, yet again, that he had a million angels working overtime on his behalf.

And that was not the last time his supreme protection would shield him from devastation. It would happen over and over again in years to come. Of course, I am ultimately thankful that nothing serious happened to him during those early days. However, while we were growing up, it pissed me off that he never seemed to fully feel the repercussions of his actions and choices. He walked away from, got off, lived through all of the harrowing situations that should have otherwise been his undoing. This *Get Out of Jail Free* pass literally said to him that he could continue on as if he were untouchable. He was like a cat with eighteen lives. He thought the supply of his freedom and charm was endless. In fact, he felt these things made him better, smarter and stronger—one degree short of the bionic man. In reality, this wide berth of freedom and lack of boundary made him more dependent, duller, and counterproductive. It seemed that, not too unlike our mother, he was also losing his way. His growing disrespect and lack of discipline nearly landed him in military academy, which in hindsight might not have been such a bad idea. However, my father strongly rejected the idea, and Parker slid by once again.

Chip and my father would soon discover that Parker's acting out was taking on a new and more upsetting turn.

It might have been Chip who first discovered tapes in Parker's room. To his and my father's utter shock, they were recordings of Parker's sexual conquests with girls moaning with pleasure and screaming out their climactic ecstasy. Needless to say, my father was mortified at hearing those tapes and dumbfounded that his son would actually record those private moments without those girls' knowledge. I'm sure Parker got a very severe tongue-lashing and *worse*, a long sober speech about my father's complete disappointment. Despite whatever the full punishment ended up being, my brother never seemed to learn from any of his poor choices. It seemed his very addiction was poor choices, if not downright *bad* choices. He couldn't kick it, couldn't break the habit.

From a distance, I became aware of a kind of alter ego or double life that he seemed determined to keep living. On the one hand, I knew him to be my cute, charming, and talented brother. On the other, as more upsetting circumstances surfaced, it unearthed hidden truths about him. Aside from his growing elusiveness, there was a kind of callousness and something detached about him. And then just as quickly, he would do or say something that would remind me of his wonderful and loving qualities. I knew him and I didn't know him. What I did know was that over and over again he continued to emerge seemingly untouched by his recklessness.

The "F" word

As Parker and I grew older, we led more separate lives. The situation of our parents' divorce, the departure of our mother from our lives, and then having two fathers as parents created an unspoken and necessary bond between us. It was a powerful and important thing that we shared. We also had many differences. Where he had embraced Chip almost instantly from the beginning, I had rejected him almost instantly. While he continued to have conversations and a connection with our mother, I rarely spoke with her or about her. Where I decided to take a more serious approach to creating a career and maintaining steady employment, Parker chose a life in the streets and maintained a mantra that the "the system" was out to get him. The system may not have minded incarcerating another young brutha with open arms to add to the steadily growing negative images of African American males in this country. However, I don't think that the system was out to keep my brother from reaching his greatest potential.

I believe he was his own worst enemy. And between the two of us, I think he had the tougher time growing up. Although he shared the more consistent and enduring bond with our mother, I believe he had a greater challenge finding his way. I came to realize that as a straight African American male, having been parented by two men was potentially an even bigger challenge to sort out than it had been for me. I know this because after years of thinking that he was fine and unaffected by our family arrangement, he told me otherwise. One day he said to me, "How could I be fine? I was a young male growing up with two men. How could I not have been affected by that?"

I told him I had no idea. I felt sadness at not having been more sensitive to the obvious. I suppose during those years I'd been too wrapped up in my own confusions. I explained to him what I'd witnessed growing up was the little boy who immediately ran into Chip's arms and always seemed accepting of his life with our father. He told me he always loved Chip, but it was still difficult to reconcile their arrangement. Chip and I were often at each other's throats, but Parker didn't seem to have many problems or confrontations. I suppose he let all of that run wild in the streets.

He always brought all of his friends over to the house in steady flow: his male friends and girlfriends alike. He showed no self-consciousness or embarrassment. I had had the opposite experience. He'd had his own challenges. He was forever the youngest and the smallest in his crowd, working hard at assuming a macho pose to appear cool with his boys, as well as walk with a secure sexuality around his girls. It wasn't until much later in his teens that a rebellion, in reaction to his locked-up feelings about Chip and our father, became evident.

Parker, Chip and I were all hanging around the laundry room doing different things. The two of them had a pissed-off exchange that I guess had to do with *too much damn laundry* and Parker never wanting to do any of his share. The tête à tête ended abruptly. But as my brother bumped past him on his way out, under his breath yet loud enough to be heard, he shot out, 'Faggot!' His delivery carried with it venomous anger and contempt. I could see the tiny imaginary daggers fly through the air to pierce one side of Chip's neck.

It was one of those moments that froze in the worst way to let the violence of the assault sink in. No one said anything. Parker hoped Chip hadn't heard although it was intended for his ears. Chip didn't want to hear what he'd just heard. And I hoped that perhaps, just perhaps, I heard it wrong. I was embarrassed for both of them, and I know that my brother regretted it. The incident was never brought up again.

But it isn't about which of us had the tougher time regarding Chip and our father or our mother, but what would we do with what we'd been dealt. We had so much in our favor. Unfortunately, with all that my brother possessed naturally as well as all of the love that was showered on him, he still managed to become the confounding statistic of a young, smart, beautiful, and talented black male gone wrong.

Despite having been born with every advantage and opportunity, he jumped the track and lost his way. My father struggled relentlessly to help Parker find his footing because he was his son and he loved him madly. He wanted him to glorify the potential that oozed out of his only gorgeous son. Instead, he saw all of that infinite possibility dripping off him and watched in horror as it gathered like muddy puddles down and around his feet to spill into the drains of those seductive streets.

My father had always given us both a great deal of freedom as young adults to make our own choices and for the most part trusted us with it. This was one of the ways in which he overcompensated for the lack of our mother. It was his way of trying to make what wasn't perfect closer to perfect. He and Chip did everything in their power to give Parker a positive sense of himself and pride in his accomplishments. Nothing seemed to help. Parker's bad judgment was becoming more financially and emotionally expensive.

Tough choices

That phone call about the Parker's car accident that came on that early morning at college happened on the same day I also would pay dearly for my own irresponsibility. My carelessness would land me hours later in a clinic, where one of my dearest friends (my Italian-Irish-American Allegra) took me to get an abortion. The many implications of what that meant wouldn't hit me until much later on in life. I do remember coming back to the apartment in Shadyside, Pittsburgh, alone, and I was stunned by just how very much alone I felt. My bedroom was sun-flooded that afternoon. Somehow when difficult or devastating events happen on bright sunny days, it makes the moment feel even more surreal. Like 9/11. We expect those events to occur when it's dark, cold, and stormy. I sat in the middle of my room on the dusty-blue carpet and silently cried. I was immeasurably and inexplicably sad.

After a little bit of time I headed straight to my voice lesson; a thing I did not relish but was resolved to do all the same. Right after that, I was off to rehearsal of an emotionally complicated original play called *Grace*. We were working on one of the hardest scenes in the story. I played the main character Grace, a young girl of fourteen whose world was turned upside-down when her father unexpectedly dies. It takes place in the South where her mother, desperate for financial security and a new man, accepts the advances of an opportunistic and morally corrupt younger man. He seduces the fourteen-year-old soon-to-be stepdaughter, and the three are caught in a volatile and sinister triangle.

It was a very difficult and somewhat disturbing project. It was also a very good and important project for me to have been involved with. I was ending my college time on a hard earned and empowering note. Graduation from C.M.U was one of the highlights of my accomplishments. It was a thing I had obtained all on my own hard work. My father and Chip were beaming and I couldn't have been more excited to have them there. They were so proud of me. *I* was so proud of me. My graduation present was a trip on my own to Europe that summer. I couldn't have asked for anything better.

At home in Holland

During that summer, I longed to spend some time working in Europe. Since coming off tour dancing, I wanted to continue, but I also knew that I didn't want to be dancing for the rest of my life. There were other things I wanted to explore. My plan was to investigate Paris and perhaps Italy, a place I'd always been especially drawn to. Unfortunately, those places were not to be part of that journey. My father had mounted a show called *A Night at the Cotton Club* in Amsterdam. It was a huge hit. Dancing and singing at The Cotton Club seemed to be my ongoing variation on a theme. Thank God. It was work. He needed an understudy for one of the leads. He offered me the job and said if I took it he would add a featured number so that I would have the opportunity to be performing each night. This way, I would not be depending solely on the nights that the lead wouldn't get on stage. It was an opportunity I couldn't turn down.

I was not only excited to be working in Europe for an extended period of time, but also to be working with my father in Europe. It was his old stomping ground and the other half of where I came from. It would be different working there together, as opposed to vacationing. Visiting Holland was always important to him. It was a part of who we were that he wanted us to remember and embrace. I was older now, and a trip to Holland with him on my own would be whole new experience. I would have my own apartment there and arrive with a bit of fanfare as the choreographer's daughter who would be joining the show. The owner of *de Telegraaf,* the city's newspaper at the time, and the producer of the show, did a lovely article on the two of us when I arrived. It had been approximately twenty years earlier that he and my mother were stars there with the Dutch National Ballet. Now Billy Wilson was returning with the next generation. It was a thrilling time for both of us. We were happy to be there together in this new way and having a great deal of fun. I eventually took on being dance captain—the person who keeps the show together once the choreographer is done creating the work, eloped with a dancer in the show, and lived there for several years before returning to New York.

Pas de deux

It was the early '90s. Before leaving for The Netherlands, my father forewarned me about a particular dancer among the cast with "slow" eyes. He would soon become my first husband. Blame it on the eyes. My father prefaced his words of caution by reminding me that he seldom interfered with my personal life, which was largely due to the fact that I scarcely had one. He said, "I know you, Holly. You'll look into his provocative eyes and melt, but I'm telling you, don't get involved. He already has a child."

Well, the proverbial elephant was taking up all space in the middle of the room before I'd even gotten on the plane to greet it in person. My curiosity was on fire.

True to my father's prediction, I was instantly intrigued and attracted. John Wooter had lived his whole life in Holland, although he was born in the South American country of Suriname, which was at one time a Dutch colony. Almost identical to me in color, with a muscular physique, he did indeed have sleepy cheaters, and his aloof personality had me rapt. That was at the age when I still considered aloofness to be a turn-on. He also happened to be easily the most talented of the dancers in the show.

Why my father chose to create a short pas de deux for John and me is something I will never understand. I guess the answer would be *just business*. We did complement one another and danced well together. We became hotly and controversially involved. It was a difficult relationship to maintain. Although John and the mother of his child had never married and had long since separated, many people connected with the show strongly disapproved of our closeness. There were times, while on tour, when we were physically separated from one another. As crazy as it sounds, we fervently believed that a few people in particular were committed to keeping the two of us apart. However, true to our ages, the more resistance we got, the more determined we were to stay together.

Ah, romance! The most difficult challenge for me to overcome, in the beginning, was the fact that my father did not support our relationship, let alone the idea of marriage. It was for the first time that father and daughter clashed with a vengeance.

My father could be incredibly stubborn. I had never before seen or felt him so completely opposed to and disappointed by a choice that I had made. As a result, I was so angry with him that it was hard for me to look him in the eyes or talk to him. This was the father I checked in with almost every day, wherever I was. For the two of us, who had been so used to constant contact, it felt very unnatural and strange. As I grew older, his perfection did not always appear perfect. All of a sudden, the disagreements were more disagreeable. I was discovering that he wasn't always right and not always in control. It was a somewhat shattering demystification of the man I'd kept sealed in the pristine curio cabinet of my mind. That awareness was not too unlike the Christmas morning I woke up to discover that the butterflies of my innocent giddy excitement, reserved for Santa Claus, had flown away. At a ripe time, my innocence was snatched away and I was left eternally changed from who I'd been. This is how I felt as I became aware of my father's humanness, his vulnerabilities, questionable choices, and sad regrets.

It was a sad period between us. It was also necessary for me to stand my ground and make my own choice in love, despite what he or anyone around me felt about it. Because there was so much tension regarding the two of us, John and I decided to elope. Although we'd only been together for six months, it was the exact choice my father made when he married my mother. I guess I was that little apple who didn't fall too far from the big tree. We had only one other couple with us, who stood as witnesses at City Hall when we made it legal.

Naturally, the elopement only made things worse. One of my favorite photos of my father and me was taken during this very difficult time between us. It was taken opening night of his musical *Josephine*, the story of Josephine Baker, in Amsterdam, when I grudgingly attended without John. The photo shows a happy moment, but in fact we were hardly speaking.

The silent treatment didn't last long between us because we were unhappy without the constant connection we'd always shared. Chip helped to mend what had been broken between us, but my father never fully accepted that union. Although Billy was not perfect, he was correct again when it came to my first choice in marriage. We weren't right for one another in many ways, and it was always messy due to the angry mother of his child. Though exciting in the beginning, the magic soon wore off after we'd taken our vows. My romantic idea of living a simple life in Europe was not quite what I'd hoped it would be. In the end we went our separate ways.

That period spent in Holland brings to mind some of the best and the worst times. It was a big part of my maturation. I left behind a girl and returned from there a young woman. And though my father, without question, had the inside track on what was best for me, I discovered that it was okay to let him know when I thought he was wrong. It was okay to disagree heatedly, be angry with him, acknowledge his not knowing everything, and live my life based on my own self-discoveries. *It's your bed; you've got to lie in it.* There's truth in that sentiment. I know that my father lived with harsh truths as well. But more than being privy to all his private failures and imperfections were the examples of an individual always striving to be better—a better artist, a better father, and a better person. I prefer to remember the sweet stuff. In our own way, we were all trying to be better and learn from what life was tossing our way. There were still miles to go, because before my time in Holland was through, I would see my mother.

Another cameo appearance

For most of my life, it was as if my mother never existed. There were a few feeble attempts at understanding one another, but we never got very far.

She and Parker continued to maintain a connection, but I wanted no part. Our conversations, if one could call them that, were very few and far between. I preferred it that way. When she would call out of the blue, I would confront her about anything and everything. Through the years she had contrived a fantasy about the part she played in our lives. She has always said she did everything for us, that she was always there, that she always tried to call, always sent things to us, was always thinking about us, but it simply wasn't true. She would pull some practiced statement out of the air and I would say, "No, you didn't; no, you haven't; no, you weren't!" She would hang up on me.

It started when I was eleven. An infrequent phone call would inevitably end up with her hanging up. The second-to-last time I saw her was shortly after my first marriage. Though still living in L.A., she was passing through Holland visiting friends. I agreed to meet her for a coffee at the train station in Rotterdam, where John and I were living.

The last time I'd seen her I was twelve. This time I was twenty-four. I had put down my guard and sword to meet her, believing that a simple cup of coffee at the station would prove harmless. I was, after all, all grown up. I could handle it—or so I thought. I'd brought pictures of the marriage day to show her. The first time I got married, I chose to wear a black dress, just as she'd done when she married my father. It may sound bizarre, but she looked very chic in her black dress. I had seen pictures and always thought it a hip choice that worked. Of course, I didn't even consciously realize that I was emulating the mother I wanted nothing to do with, yet I'd brought evidence that proved my attempt to be close to her in some way. She looked at the photos and took note of my dress by saying, "You wore black on your wedding day. It will never last." Devastated, I picked up my photos and left her standing there in the middle of that bustling train station all by herself. That was close to twenty years ago.

The end of the affair

Many things had begun to turn sour for me in Holland. My young marriage was declining, and the producers weren't supporting my efforts to maintain my father's show my way. My failing self-esteem turned into a string of disappointments. I was trying to make a life on my terms and sometimes that can be lonely and disillusioning. They say to be careful what you wish for, and those are grossly understated words. I drifted further and further away from dancing. I wasn't enjoying it anymore. I was soon out of shape, losing my speed, and losing my desire. It's too hard a life if you don't love it.

I loved dancing and I hated it. That, in a nutshell, was my affair with it. It was always a love/hate relationship. I fear that I loved dancing mostly because it came naturally to me. I loved the feeling of being on stage, the applause, the frantic energy of pulling it all together: the "theater" of it. The goal of meeting the demands of the next project or piece of choreography, when accomplished, was a great feeling and a real boon to my self-image. Somewhere in the ease of dancing, for me, was a challenge that I liked. Perhaps I wasn't challenged enough. It seems I was pulled with a greater force into complacency and into a reluctance to push past the ease. Easy, easy, easy. Easy to coast, easy to fool some people, easy to expect less of myself, but all disastrous for any design on being great.

Early on, the idea of becoming great was just that, an idea. However, the reality of what was really required was far too uncomfortable and scary. I was able to move from work to other work, on the surface. The person I know I never fooled was my father. He knew what I was capable of, and he never let me slide. There was nothing about his approach to the work or to his life that revolved around doing anything because it was easy. I knew this in my head, but I couldn't allow all of me to surrender. Maybe it was too messy, too unbridled, and too raw, or required me to be more uninhibited. It was all of these.

There were isolated moments, usually while working with him, when I did lose myself and go to the next place. It is that scary place that all committed artists must go to be revealed, to evolve, and be reborn. That place where you're always pushing the envelope in an effort to inch ever closer to being authentic. The place where one is required to be uncomfortable and to feel as though one might die. It is then an almost holy experience.

The other side of that scary place is total freedom. It reminds me of a course that was offered in college that so intrigued me, called "Sex and Death." It is ying and yang, love and hate, ecstasy and expiration. It is true passion. The great ones reveal this, whether it is in the precision of a life-threatening operation, the finessing of a sweet deal, the soaring note of a heavenly voice, or the royal bow of a great dancer. It is to me, the essence of life at its very best.

For me, it was too unsafe. My salvation would not come with dancing. It would not come with acting, although I believed I was getting closer. It would be writing that would introduce me to myself. I discovered later it was that other thing that I thought I might want to spend the rest of my life doing. Writing is the thing in many ways that saved me. It saved me from hiding from myself, from my world, and from my life.

Perhaps, dancing saved me in ways that I didn't recognize at the time. Regardless of my fight with it, it also has given me great joy. It brought me to my body in the best ways. It introduced me to a sensuality and delicious-ness that is unlike anything else when it's right. It has given me a discipline that I have taken with me and have used in every aspect of my life. It has given me a profound appreciation of the human form, in all its variety and limitless possibilities. My dancing life brought me opportunities and experi-ences that have been sweet and wonderful. I would change nothing. All of this has made me who I am. I look at the memories of dancing as I would a cherished lover—one I have adored but with whom I could never stay.

CHAPTER 10

THE BEGINNING OF THE END

WHILE I TRIED to grow up a little bit more, Chip started having trouble with his career. He was struggling to realize his dream of being a commercial success in the music industry. It seemed the universe had another path for him to travel. Despite the universe's plan, he still wanted that thing which seemed forever out of reach. The final blow came in the form of a record contract disappointment.

A man by the name of Dick Scott had a little something to do with a devastating outcome of career events. He was the mastermind behind New Kids On The Block. In the late '80s, it was one of the first chart-topping all-white boy bands that tried their hand at singing like brown boys. Chip had known Dick for some time before all the success of New Kids. My guess is that he misled Chip. Dick had always given him the impression that he would get him out there to become the next Luther Vandross. To some extent, my father and I both felt that perhaps Chip had been born in the wrong era. It's a rather lame excuse for a complex question of "What happened?" We would wonder what if he'd come along in the '50's or '60s, in the time of Billy Eckstine and Johnny Hartman? Would his voice have been a gold mine *then*? Instead, there he was in the '80s and '90s, when Michael Jackson's high-pitched falsetto became synonymous with "the King of Pop," while Kool and the Gang and Lionel Richie were the commercial balladeers of the day. We'd left Issac Hayes, Barry White, and Teddy Pendergrass long behind. At the time Chip was actively pursuing his commercial dream, that particular black male vocal train had, for the most part, left the station. Chip liked the phrase *timing is everything,* but perhaps he'd miscalculated. Perhaps his own timing was a little bit off or the industry just wasn't ready for him. Regardless, the talent was special. Chip was gifted, and it's a sad loss that more people didn't have the opportunity to hear that gorgeous voice.

Hearing him was like journeying down a warm, rich, thick slide of dark bittersweet chocolate. The more you rolled it around in your ears, the headier it became, like expensive brandy. His voice was a mighty cloud that thundered, that raised you high and then brought you down as if it had all been a dream because the ride was so smooth, so gentle, and so easy. He had bedroom eyes and a bedroom voice. His notes hung on and kept you rapt. These were facts that could not be denied. What also could not be denied was a failed promise made to Chip by Mr. Scott.

The record contract he was promised—the contract that was supposed to catapult Chip into the stratosphere of commercial stardom—never happened. When it didn't materialize the second time, it broke his heart. The first time, he was younger and able to bounce back from the disappointment with a fiery determination. This last time, when he was in his 40s, it left him in emotional chaos. "What happens to a dream deferred?" asked the poet Langston Hughes. It was Chip's last chance at the brass ring. In the wake of a lost dream, what predisposes one individual never to lose heart and the other to wither into mental breakdown? Chip's depression was great and by the time he was in Europe performing in my father's show, the dam was breaking.

Things fall apart

In a photo taken in his dressing room, Chip's wide, frightened eyes told the story of what was on the way. By the time they were early into the run of the show, he broke out with shingles and his behavior became more and more unsettling. My father had encouraged him, after the record label disaster, to step into one of the leads in *A Night at the Cotton Club* to get his mind on something else. This was one of two shows that my father had running in Amsterdam at the same time. The other show was *Josephine*. Unfortunately, there was at least one person in *Cotton Club* who was driven to break Chip, even though he was already in a broken and vulnerable state. All he needed was a gentle tug at the fabric of what was precariously keeping him together to have the whole garment unravel before our eyes.

And that's just what happened. He unraveled, came unglued, broke down, and slowly checked out. It began with that wildness in his eyes. They became too bright, too wide, too alert, and his handwriting became smaller, almost microscopic, and visibly shaken. The next tell was his extravagant buying of things in multiple quantities. Instead of buying one Chambray 75 Euro Oxford shirt, he bought six. He bought hats with hatboxes, silk scarves and ties, cufflinks, and socks. He had become obsessed with shopping in this excessive way. Next came the voices. He heard voices in his head telling him a variety of unsettling things. One voice told him to begin work on creating a new show, while another whispered about a conspiracy to kill him.

Parker was the first to let my father and me know what was going on. Parker was in Europe with Chip. My father succeeded in wooing Parker as well, as a last attempt to keep him on the straight and narrow, to use his dancing talent by offering him a job as a dancer in the show. Parker accepted the challenge. He worked hard in preparation to do what would be required. Before going over to Europe, he watched tapes of the show day and night to become familiar with the choreography. He hadn't danced since he was a child but, true to form, he picked it up like a pro and ended up being terrific in the show. It seemed the perfect situation for both Parker and Chip to be working together, making some money, and away from circumstances that had negative or destructive holds on them.

However, early in the run, Parker was concerned about Chip's behavior. He phoned my father, telling him how nasty some of the cast members were towards Chip. What had begun with a single toxic influence was quickly turning into a clique of several cast members seemingly out for Chip's blood. There was more than enough theater to go around, both on and off stage. This extra drama only made Chip's mental state worse. Soon came phone calls from the producers of the show, expressing concern about Chip's bizarre behavior.

I was no longer with that show but was still living in Holland. Though my father was back in the States during this time, we spoke regularly on the phone. On a break during their tour, my father flew back to Holland, knowing almost certainly that Chip was in the throes of a nervous break-down and Dad would need to get him back home immediately. He didn't, however, know just how difficult that would be.

The three of them—Chip, Parker and my father—were back in Amsterdam all staying in a flat together. Parker would call me in the middle of the night to report that Chip couldn't calm down enough to sleep and couldn't stop talking. He was keeping them up all night long. Aware of his own unstoppable chatter, Chip taped his mouth with duct tape in an effort to be quiet. My father and brother were so exhausted and so sad for Chip. They couldn't leave him alone in the apartment and they couldn't let him roam the streets by himself for fear of his becoming disoriented, lost, or worse. They had to hide certain objects, sharp things in particular, not knowing what he might do. They weren't as afraid for their own safety as they were for his, especially since the white devils, as he called them, were getting louder and more persuasive in his mind. Sometimes they had to take turns staying up with him or literally lock him in the bedroom in an effort to get some sleep. Only utter exhaustion would finally force Chip's 6'2" frame to drop like a rock into a nap, at odd times; then he'd be up and in his manic state all over again. His mind wouldn't or couldn't shut off.

He was becoming more and more paranoid and convinced that these demons were out to destroy him. He started counting numbers constantly, writing things down furiously, and making lists. He would only wear certain colors and had adopted all kinds of unusual rituals. None of these rituals could be disturbed or he would erupt into a rage. My father found a doctor in Holland who was able to help. He'd made a couple of house calls to give Chip a look and administer something to help him sleep, but it was clear he needed to be admitted for serious treatment. Getting him on the plane for home would prove a challenge. That trip home was inching closer, and my father, along with the doctor, concluded that the only way to get Chip there was to have him sedated with a tranquilizer to keep him knocked out for most of the flight. Thank God, heavy security checks at the airports were not yet in full swing, which would have only added to their nightmare. My father was dreading the voyage, but at least Parker would be on the flight to help. I was planning to go back to be with them when I could make that arrangement. But before they would make their journey, we all met, includ-ing Chip, in the evening for dinner at a Chinese restaurant in the middle of Amsterdam.

Last supper

It was a very difficult meal. I'd finally gotten the opportunity to witness firsthand what Parker and our father had been dealing with. That dinner was, in a word, scary. The need for conversation got trapped in our throats and food was simply reshuffled on all of our plates. Chip's plate remained empty. None of us had an appetite. It was a horribly surreal family night. Chip talked incessantly about everything from white devils to the extravagant theater productions he was in the midst of creating. He would spontaneously duck this way and that, as if someone or something were swatting at him. He told us that those were the devils flying around him. He was dressed only in black and red with a huge black Borsolino hat that he never took off. My father tried to keep him calm and reassured. Luckily, the four of us sat upstairs in the restaurant where we were alone.

At times Chip was funny about something cryptic and true; then he would turn on a dime and retell the first time he met us at the house on West Brookline Street. He talked about me, how I stood there judging him coldly in my ten-year-old body. He would all at once lay into one of us. Then his attention would shift and someone else would end up on his chopping block. He was exposing our imperfections, our faults, and flaws. The things he revealed were often true but things a mindful and considerate person would never say. It was completely uncensored. Chip would reach into us and expose the very thing we didn't want revealed, discussed, or discovered. He disrobed our dark sides. His grocery list of assaults left us feeling naked and shameful. The three of us looked from one to the other, hoping for forgiveness and wishing for a spaceship to fly us out of the moment, out into orbit and any place other than where we were. We sat there afraid of so many things.

At the end of this so-called dinner, I said my good-byes to Parker and Chip. I searched Chip's eyes for something familiar. All I saw was sadness and vacancy. No one was home. Parker walked Chip downstairs. He had a way with him during this period. Chip trusted Parker it seemed, more than anyone else.

My father lingered behind upstairs with me. He then looked into my eyes as he rested his hand, both gingerly and heavily, onto my arm to say, "Holly, I don't know what to do," and dissolved into a river of tears. I had never seen him weep in that way. My strong, powerful, invincible father was transformed into a scared and lost little boy before my eyes. All I could do was hold onto him as I felt the tremors of his crying against me. I had no answer, no sage advice, and no way out.

We walked slowly towards the exit to lead us down the stairs, amid a Chinese clatter and Dutch language that swirled senselessly around us; it was like walking to face execution. I don't think we were sure just whose it would be. My father didn't want to face it. He walked as if through mud and sand and dark molasses. Dread walked with him, but I also walked with him. And though I would not be leaving with them on that flight back to the new house in Teaneck, New Jersey, I decided in that moment that I would be there soon, as soon as I could. My father needed me and I would be there.

For the first few days following their departure, I walked around Amsterdam amid canals and brightly colored tulips in a fog, with a sense of knowing that a part of my world, of our world, our family, would be forever changed. Ironically, Chip and I had so recently found the real love and friendship between us—and all of a sudden it seemed to be blowing up in billowing grey smoke.

Dad, Parker, and Chip did make it home, with Chip heavily tranquilized, on an interminable flight. We spoke on the phone constantly, trying to buoy one another's spirits and gather our Wilson strength as I made plans to return home. The length of my stay would remain unclear until Chip was relatively on his way to getting the help he needed. My father still had commitments, contracts to fulfill, and magic to create. The work still demanded his time and energy, and so did the bills waiting for him on his desk. Meanwhile, arriving back at the house in Teaneck was like entering a war zone, a black hole, and a slippery slope of what had become Chip's growing insanity.

The normal, everyday scenarios didn't stop coming just because Chip was having a nervous breakdown. On the sidelines, at the house on Cedar Lane, we were each struggling with our own personal dramas.

Wake up!

Another sight for this daughter's sore eyes is a reflection upon a summer day when my father was strong and healthy. It was I again who needed his caretaking. I had recently returned home to help since Chip's mental breakdown.

Although my relationship with John, my ex, was very passionate in the beginning, the union was mostly wrong from the start. The strain over our differences had pushed us further apart. We came from different socioeconomic backgrounds, had a different work ethic, and our goals for the future were also not completely on the same page.

Despite all that, I was spreading my wings and determined to do it my way. John and I agreed that I should return to the States, not only to be of help to my father, but also to make sure I wasn't missing out on something in the business. More and more of my friends were steadily working in film and TV, while I was losing momentum in Holland. We both decided that after a few months back in the States I would discover something or nothing. I would return to Holland and we'd take it from there. Perhaps he would come to the States? I honestly believe it was fate giving me the opportunity, under the guise of searching for something else, that brought me to the ultimate truth—the ultimate truth being that although we'd once been very much in love, it was over.

Unfortunately, it took a trip across a rather large ocean for me to make this important discovery and with little help from my husband. After being back in the States for nearly three months, I hadn't received so much as a postcard from him. Although we spoke at length daily, usually at my expense, he seemed to be having no difficulty with our distance apart. One day, in passing, I mentioned this to my father.

"Dad, you know John hasn't written me once since I've been here." I was writing John two and three times a day. We were still so young in our marriage, and the separation for me was excruciating.

"Not even a postcard?" he asked. I shook my head. "That doesn't make any sense, Holly. You mean to tell me that your husband, the man who's supposed to be crazy about you, has not so much as been reminded of *anything* that makes him think of you; some postcard, some something? Oh no. Something is very wrong. And you've been writing him like mad and making all these phone calls."

I, of course, went on to defend this impossible situation. *He's busy, he doesn't really like to write, the aromas from the Dutch tulips have been so overwhelming this season, he can't think straight.* All of the many pathetic excuses only a fool in love makes when she feels she's losing him.

"I really think he's back with that woman again," my father said.

"What woman? Yolanda? No."

"He's had a child with this woman, Holly."

"I know." My hurt was all being dragged up into my throat. The rest of my body was shrinking around it, like an inner vacuum. For months I'd walked around with this strain, this constant tightness in my heart, hoping it would all resolve itself in a fairy-tale way. But something *was* wrong. What was happening or had happened? What had I done or not done? I confronted him one last time by phone. He said that nothing was wrong. Now I was really in a spin because I didn't think John was being honest with me. I could hardly concentrate on anything. I baked cakes at my father's house to keep my mind preoccupied, and I was also trying to re-establish my long-standing relationship with Abrams Artists, the very supportive agents I'd had since C.M.U. Trying to get back on the scene, as it were.

My heart wasn't really in it. I was behind. I hadn't been dancing or acting, and when I walked into auditions, it was disconcerting not to be familiar with any of the up and comings. It wasn't important, but it added to my sense of loneliness. I believe my spirit had broken a bit in Holland. My desire for performing had left me. Despite all that, I was trying. I knew that one of the ways to survive the strain of whatever was happening between John and me was to work and keep busy.

"Holly, if you believe in this marriage and if you love him, maybe you need to go back there and find out what's going on ... if you want to save it." This was very unusual advice coming from my father—the man who'd warned me not to get involved with John before I'd even gotten on the plane to go to Holland and join the show. I know it was hard for him to see his child in pain. It was the very thing he'd spent his life as a parent trying to protect me from. Before I'd even met the man I would marry, he had seen the inevitable handwriting on the wall.

Confronting John on the phone had not helped to bring the truth of what was happening between us to the surface. I wrote a long letter, essentially letting him off the hook. In it I said that it seemed obvious to me that our marriage was failing and also that he seemed disinclined to help save it. Therefore, the obvious choice seemed to be to have our marriage annulled. It was one of the most difficult letters I've ever written. People don't go into marriage expecting it to end in divorce. I wanted to give it a chance and to give my best at that chance. One person cannot overcome the challenges of two, alone.

I almost immediately received a letter back—the first he'd sent since we'd been apart. It was as if he'd been waiting for me to say what he perhaps could not. At the time, I could only call him a bastard and be furious with myself for marrying a man with "no balls." He'd written back to say yes, it was true, let's end this—and with no more explanation than that. I was shocked, then devastated and finally, relieved. The worst of it was not knowing. Once you know what you're up against, it's easier to fight for it or leave it behind you. There was one last phone call between us. When I got off the phone, I vomited and cried for the rest of that day.

Parker offered to fly overseas and knock him out, break his legs, or something to that effect. It was tempting but I declined. The gesture, though not the most appropriate choice, made me cry as well because I knew how much my brother loved me and wanted to protect me. That feeling was priceless. I was staying at my dear friend Cynthia's apartment in the city at the time of that last phone call. I was alone except for the dog, Chloe. I needed to be "home." The heart of retelling this story lies in the love and concern that was waiting for me there. The next morning I called my father.

"He wants a divorce".

"Hmm." Long pause. "Do you want to come home?"

"Yes."

"Do you need me to pick you up?"

"No, that's okay, I'll take the bus. I'll be there soon." Long pause again.

"You all right, Holly?"

"I love you, Dad."

"I love you too, Beauty. Come home. We're here. Don't worry." He took a beat. "Let's face it, he's a real creep." We both chuckled. My throat caught. It was an inside joke that took the edge off.

All I could think of at that moment was thank God for my father. Thank God he's here. Thank God I'm home. That morning was bright and sunny. When life happens to shatter your seemingly safe and somewhat predictable world, after you've cried your eyes out and gut- wrenching sounds are released from the pit of your stomach, the planet feels changed. Of course, the world has gone on; spinning just the same, but something in you has changed, shifted. That morning on the bus, I looked out at all of the houses and trees I knew almost by heart and saw them anew. At times I was seeing right through them. Sometimes I saw nothing but the movie reels of the last three years playing over and over in my head. Searching for some clue. Trying to make sense of it. Yet in between my steady flow of tears, even then, I had seconds, minutes, and moments of thankfulness behind the hurt. I knew that eventually this would lead me to a better and stronger place. I was going home.

I took the local bus. I wanted to take a long ride. The bus stopped at the bottom of a steep hill that led to our house in Teaneck. That walk felt like moving through thick mud. My body was now carrying the burden of disappointment and disbelief. I was almost to the house. About three or four more houses away. I saw my father. I breathed in deeply and exhaled sadness. I got closer—and breathed in relief and exhaled familiarity. He waved. He had been riding his bike. Had a baseball cap on his head. I got closer. I breathed in safety and exhaled joy at seeing my father's face. I breathed in failure and exhaled *sorry, I should have listened to you Dad.* I breathed in feeling so scared and exhaled *what am I going to do?* Two feet in front of him, I took a quick breath in. I looked into his watery eyes and began to sob in his arms. I couldn't stop and I couldn't speak. He put his bike down sideways on the lawn without letting me go and we walked into the house.

"You'll be all right. I'll run you a hot bath and give you half a Valium. It will help you sleep. It'll be all right. I'm so glad you're home." I, too, was so glad to be home and in the loving safety, familiar smells, inescapable laughter, and irreplaceable arms of my father. All of this and with no "I told you so." I was home. I would heal. I felt blessed to have a father who would always be there to make things better. However, I couldn't wallow too long in my own emotional muck and mire. We had to get Chip better as soon as possible.

Show time

Chip's latest preoccupation was contacting performers in *the business* for the upcoming show he was creating. However, he was creating it only in his own mind. He was constantly summoning us to sit down and listen to his many ideas, notes, and scene changes. In his mind his show *was* happening. My father found himself running interference with all the many calls Chip made, inviting people to either be a part of or to attend the opening of his fantasy. Those phone calls ranged from the neighbor walking his dog to Lena Horne and everyone else in between. Not only was my father scrambling to apologize profusely to each individual and assure them no such show existed, he was simultaneously forced to expose the devastating reality of things.

Chip was calling everyone he knew, my father knew, and some they didn't. Even a few who were no longer living received a call. Among those on the list were Cab Calloway, Chita Rivera, Dianne Carrol, Hugh Wheeler, Eartha Kitt, Hal Prince, and Sidney Poitier. For those whom he'd never met or who had already departed, he was just as thrilled to speak with a relative, assistant or former lover. Some picked up the phone; thankfully, others did not. It was a difficult and embarrassing fix for my father. All the while, Chip was ordering fabrics for costumes, assembling costumers and assistants, as well as parading in endless costumes of his own. At times he would be outrageously funny and all at once tragically sad.

On the first day Chip was to be admitted to St. Vincent's psychiatric wing to be evaluated for meds, he came down the stairs in full phantasmagoria. He'd been up in his room the whole morning preparing. It's of some importance to remember that Michael Jackson at that time was at the peak of oversaturation by the media. Chip descended in all black, except for a blood red dress shirt, shiny patent leather dress shoes, an Italian fedora cocked expertly over one eye, an enormous scarf draped around his shoulders like a cape, full make-up complete with a red high gloss to his full lips ... and one white glove. Michael Jackson meets Zorro. He was, in essence, ready for his close-up, Mr. DeMille. We watched him float down the staircase in utter disbelief, but none of us were about to upset his applecart. He got into the car with my father and drove down the Palisades to meet the doctor on 13th Street. He was, without a doubt, going to the right place. All we could think was "poor Chip," but at the same time, we got a chuckle of endearment seeing him go out with style and with showbiz. A bit over the top, but it was pure theater—the thing we all loved so much.

I believe that Chip was actually admitted that day as he walked through St. Vincent's doors. The days, weeks, and months that followed were a barrage of upsetting surprises and shocking occurrences. From then on, he continued in and out of the hospital on a fairly regular basis, sometimes for a few days, sometimes for many weeks, for close to a year. They gave him many opportunities to attempt leading a normal life at home as an outpatient. The sad and exasperating fact was that he wouldn't take his meds. He hid them, he lied, and he threw them across the floor. On another day—a *good* day—he was cooperative and sweet as can be.

He was diagnosed with having bipolar disorder—one moment manic, the next depressed. Some of the saddest moments, due to heavy doses of lithium, were when he was sedated. On those days, the house would be as still as the calm before a storm. He'd spend all day upstairs, on the top floor with the black and white tiles leading to his bed and just sit staring out of the window. He was quiet then. We could rest a bit. Our world stopped spinning out of control for a time. It allowed us to exhale, instead of holding our breath and hoping we wouldn't pass out. We couldn't pass out. During those more peaceful moments was also when Chip was least like himself. No big hysterical laugh, no playin' the dozens, no smart-ass remarks or grand ideas, no plots to hatch or hidden agendas. He was just … quiet. Then, when whatever it was that inspired him to stop taking his meds, all hell broke loose. Doctors spent months trying to find the right levels to keep the chemicals in his brain stabilized. Until that time, his highs remained in the stratosphere and in his lows, he seemed lobotomized.

Trying to keep up with a loved one who is bipolar is in a category all its own. Because Chip was a 6' 2" male, there were times when we feared his strength. He was also manipulative and wily. He would tell outrageous untruths about each of us in an effort to pit us against one another, which caused even more tension. We had to watch him like a hawk. If we didn't, he would walk out the door and return carrying four bags of bibles, with a big smile on his face and a twinkle in his eyes as he clutched his holy offerings. It was hard then to be angry with him. At other times, we were so furious with his escapades that we were on the verge of losing *our* minds. For months we continued to find bibles hidden in every room of the house. So many scenes with Chip, so many bizarre and painful memories as he steadily lost his way. There are two vivid memories that stick out in particular.

Chip's universe

The first time I went to visit Chip while he was in the psychiatric wing at St. V's hospital, was nothing short of walking through a silver screen and onto the corridors of *One Flew Over the Cuckoo's Nest*. Seeing that movie is reliving the reality of what it was like to visit another universe. I stood in the elevator with my father, not knowing what to expect. I don't think we ever came to see Chip empty-handed. My father brought him either a favorite cozy wool sweater or a bar of chocolate, which he coveted. We brought him good food to eat, which we knew would be of comfort to him. On the way downtown from New Jersey, we would go to Wilson's soul food restaurant in Harlem to pick him up some smothered pork chops with rice, collard greens, cornbread, yams, and peach cobbler. We also couldn't resist bringing home a sweet potato pie for ourselves. Those foods brought him such happiness. He wasn't so "crazy" that he'd pass up some good food.

The small elevator door opened, and we walked out onto a long grey hallway of dull white, cold, hard floors, and faces. It was positively surreal. As soon as we stepped out of the elevator, they greeted us. The patients. The displaced, the misplaced, the misunderstood— belligerent and docile human beings flooded us with every manner of expression. Some said, "Welcome," while others proclaimed, "Fuck you!" They grabbed, stroked, giggled, and smiled. We had stepped into their world and there were different rules. There were certain things you could not bring in and certain patients you left alone. Some told elaborate stories or repeated a single phrase over and over; some kept to themselves while others instigated small daily riots. I remember one patient in particular.

I'll call her Maggie. She was a tiny, jumpy, young Latina with a mane of thick, black, wild hair. Maggie would run up to meet us. She was very sweet and acted like a little girl, though she was clearly considerably older. She would ask us for a candy bar. Even when I came back and forth a couple times in one day, she would ask me as if for the first time. I would try to bring her a bar each time we came. We later found out from Chip's doctor that Maggie had an agenda. As soon as I would give her the candy, she would disappear. We learned that she was hoarding them underneath her mattress, along with a variety of other hot items. Turns out, she was a certified kleptomaniac. She had asked for candy, but she was stealing anything else she could get her hands on. If you missed a comb or a pen while visiting, chances were pretty damn good that Maggie and her sticky fingers had something to do with it. It was an infuriating situation, especially for her fellow patients, but her sweetness made you instantly forget it had ever happened.

As unsettling as the visits to Chip were, on many levels, we imagined what Chip was feeling and fearing. He was without question the star of the floor. All the patients on Rice 5 flocked to Chip like moths to a flame. They came to him for advice and to beg him to sing another song. There was a black upright piano on the floor. Someone played and Chip would entertain. There, he had all the time in the world to put all of his creative ideas in motion and without having to pay anyone a salary—a producer's dream. His new friends would dance around giggling and smiling to a tune that temporarily made that floor a happy place.

Visiting there, especially when the snow was falling, made me think about how all of New York and the planet were buzzing by with all their feast and famine, while these delicate individuals were completely untouched by it all. They were, indeed, in their own private world. And there were many moments when my father and I got pulled into that world whether we wanted to or not, like the time we lost Chip and the car in the same night.

Winter in Lisbon

It was the longest night. One of the longest nights in my three years of emotional chaos, and a night I will never forget. Once again Chip needed to be admitted to St. Vincent's Hospital. He had been in and out of the hospital so many times that everyone there called him by his first name. It was on a weekend during a cold winter month, and it took us all day to get him in there. I can recall the wind whipping around us downtown as we struggled to keep Chip steady. St. Vincent's sits cemented on a corner that's like a magnet for wind—like Riverside Drive on the Hudson River or Lake Michigan pulling on the Miracle Mile. As clear as that day was, it was bitter and unforgiving. When Chip was finally admitted, my father and I went home exhausted. It was around 11:00 p.m. I got into bed straight from the car. These episodes were frequent but we never got used to the strain of it all. At that time, no one was feeling the strain more than my father. He was going to bed with the TV on when the phone rang.

I had nearly fallen asleep, and yet it was always the half-awake kind of sleep that descends when someone you love is in trouble. During that time, there was always fear. Certain drama or trauma seemed just around the bend. At midnight, my father woke me up from my half-sleep. He said that Mr. Carter, a handyman who did some repairs and watched the house when we were away, had just called. Mr. Carter said that Chip had just been by in a limo but didn't stay. My father told Mr. Carter that Chip was in the hospital in New York, so there must be some mistake. However, Mr. Carter assured my father that it was Chip, and that he was dressed only in a bathrobe and hospital slippers.

When I think of hospitals now, I am constantly reminded of those foam Kelly-green slippers that never stay on the patients' feet and wonder how someone decided that these would be a comfort. Did that same person conclude that they would actually keep a person's feet warm on those cold hospital floors? Those icy grey floors also bring to mind the smells. The smell of canned string beans, cauliflower, the smell of antiseptic, urine, plastic trays, and stolen cigarettes that mingle with the sickening and invisible sweet smell of creeping death. Once you've lived with these smells, like the haunting scenarios that have led you there, they never leave you. It only takes the sight of a hospital or the mention of a needle to bring it all flooding back.

When my father hung up the phone, we looked at each other in shock and disbelief. It just couldn't be! Then again, we had journeyed through many incredible, shocking, and heartbreaking months with Chip. My father called the hospital. He was on hold for a long time while they checked on Chip. Meanwhile, our hearts were in our throats, feeling as though we might possibly be on the brink of living a situation that movies are made of. I remember by this time my father was sitting on the right side of the bed with the clean starched sheets turned down, the bright bedside light turned on, sputter coming from the TV, and deafening silence inside our heads as we held our breath. I stood beside him ... waiting.

When he heard, "He's not in his room, Mr. Wilson," my father proceeded to give the hospital what for. I told him to call Jimmy at Allstate Limo. My father had an account with Allstate, and it was possible Chip had ordered a car.

Yes, Chip had ordered a car and asked the driver to take him to Englewood, New Jersey, where we used to live. Jimmy dispatched the driver, who said he'd just dropped Chip off in front of Baumgart's Restaurant. I called. It was a shot in the dark at that hour. Someone picked up. No, no one had seen a 6'2" black man standing outside the restaurant in a robe, looking disoriented. "

Almost immediately the phone rang again, making us both jump. It was the Englewood police. They had Chip, and could we please come down to the station to pick him up?

We flew out of our warm, safe home into the chilling cold night air and back into the car. Where was Parker when we needed him? My father and I were both very quiet on the ride to Englewood, hoping that Chip was unharmed and not too cold. How warm could he possibly be with the little he had on in twenty-degree weather? My father threw the multicolored afghan in the trunk. Chip's grandmother had crocheted it for him. I still have it. It has a white background with many Aztec-like shapes thrown all over it like confetti. It is bordered in green, brown and purple. Chip loved that afghan! It had become his security blanket.

There he was. His hair looked like peach fuzz on a baby chick, only it was black mixed with patches of grey. The illness and the drugs had given his hair that familiar look, a look that I'd come to recognize over and over and still over again. Today when I walk down the streets of New York in particular and spot a very gaunt, painfully thin, and shaky individual making his or her way valiantly across the street, I look at the hair.

That childlike disarray of short, soft spikes. It is also in the cheeks. It is in the dark medicated color of the skin and in the eyes. His eyes were wide like that of a frightened and helpless animal. He was shivering and his teeth were chattering. His body, the once beautifully sculpted physique, was rapidly becoming a shadow of what it once was. We used to laugh and marvel at how he would sink to the bottom of a swimming pool because his muscle mass was so dense. He would sink like a glistening brown brick. His tiny waist was a sight that both men and women gasped at and the likes of which accentuated his Nubian-like frame. The washboard stomach that rippled and all the rest had rapidly turned to brown, ashen clay. Only his magnificently enormous hands, those beautiful and expressive hands, didn't shrink or lose their strength until later. Later, his hands and feet blew up like fat, round, brown tomatoes, swollen and unfamiliar.

We both cried inside. I could see in my father's eyes that he was tearing at the seams from the stress of it all—little by little, day by day, and hour by hour. I looked at him and knew how he longed to make it all better, to make all the hurt go away, to not feel so powerless, and at those most painful moments to change places with him if he could. My father wrapped the afghan around Chip, we thanked the policemen, took in a deep breath and at nearly 1 a.m. made our way back into Manhattan to St. Vincent's for a second try.

On the way in, we prayed to get there without incident. This meant without Chip's jumping out of the car, which was not out of the realm of possibility for someone in a manic state. Luckily, and to our surprise, Chip had fallen fast asleep in the back seat of my father's comfortable deep-navy town car. That car sometimes seemed to be the glue that held it all together. In good times, it was my father's pride and joy and immediate freedom. In not-so-good times, it was our lifeline, our lifeboat, and the one thing we could count on to get us from A to B.

It's funny how nothing expensive or grand seems very grand or important when life's putting you through it. It makes the bumps a bit softer and the ride a bit smoother, but it doesn't make the pain go away. As we neared the hospital, Chip woke up, and realizing where we were headed, started to get agitated. It was freezing at 2 a.m. All we had to do was go about two blocks to get Chip back into the hospital.

He was really getting upset, and once out of the car, headed in the opposite direction. My father tried to coax him but Chip became more and more angry. Then he started swinging. We couldn't get near him. My father was running down the middle of a deserted 7th Avenue after this big black man with nothing on but a robe, foam slippers falling off, and a multi-colored afghan covering his head. He looked like any crazy on the streets of New York.

But it wasn't just any nameless, faceless, or homeless man on the streets. In the middle of the night, my father was running after Chip. Chip, who'd gotten him through the insanity of the divorce, the backaches, too much Valium, and a teenaged daughter who did everything in her painful and confused power to make him miserable. The same Chip who hung in there through all of it, who wiped our runny noses, baked us homemade strawberry shortcake for our birthdays, picked up my brother from Little League, and sewed my denim dress on his brand-new sewing machine. God, how I wish I'd saved that dress, for now I would truly appreciate it! My father was running after this beautiful man, this talented man who was his best friend and soul mate. The person he shared his dreams with, his children, and his life for eighteen years

It was getting colder. At this point, there was no getting Chip anywhere near the hospital. My father told me to call the police. Luckily, there happened to be a van full of cops pulling up across the street. I ran over and asked for help. The two of us were now walking on opposite sides of the street watching, as five policemen talked to Chip and eventually coaxed him into walking through the Emergency doors.

We sat in Emergency for another hour while they put us through the insufferable red tape of bureaucratic bullshit to get him readmitted. While we waited, Chip was getting into a good humor. He was increasingly aware of the familiar hospital "audience." At first he sat quietly like an obedient little boy with his head down, knees together, and palms flat on his thighs. All at once he began to sing "Alfie" in full voice. For a while he sang from his seat, then it took him up to standing and he was off ... through the corridors and to the nurses' station. Many of the nurses knew Chip and consequently didn't pay him much attention, except to compliment him on how well he sounded that night.

It was a bittersweet scene. Despite the sad reality of his bipolar condition, one had to respect the sincerity of his conviction. Chip loved performing and craved the fame and fortune that had eluded him. When the song was over, he proceeded to make sure everyone there was aware that they were in the presence of God. He told people they should get on their knees and bow while in *his* presence and gave each person an imaginary number. Numbers had become of increasing importance to him. He was in rare form that night and very funny. He was "reading" people—giving them what for—left, right and center, and finding a cruel pleasure in it. No one in Emergency was spared; not the man with his head covered in blood or the middle-aged woman on a gurney screaming and gripping her stomach in pain. In an odd way it lightened our night, and we were happy to see Chip laughing. He was no longer angry or despondent. He was an entertainer, and he was indeed very entertaining at this point of the late black night. By this time, it was nearly early morning, and it was not yet over.

Chip's mood swings had taken him to a better place for now. These swings came and went, and we did our best to swing with them. At one point, after he had gone back to the cracked orange seat, after the song, two police officers were passing by on their way out; they were burly and New York cynical. As they were passing, we were watching Chip watching them and knew that something was on the way. Chip looked at them with exaggerated disgust and said, "Here they come with *their* macho bullshit." Well, everyone within earshot broke out laughing. Even the cops had to chuckle and shrugged it off New York-style as they left. Where had *that* come from? However, within the manic state and the heightened behavior came the things we recognized as beautifully Chip.

By the time we left Emergency and knew that he was safely tucked away, we went back out into the night air and were again slapped by the reality of the world outside of Chip's world. We were now feeling our exhaustion and were eager to make our way back home so that we might finally be in for the night. We walked around the corner to where we'd parked the car but the car had disappeared. It was nowhere to be found. We thought we were losing our minds and that the weight of our recently immobilizing fatigue was making us come to this impossible conclusion. But the car really was gone. In fact, it had been towed. I believe we found this out from a graveyard-shift doorman who witnessed the abduction. We were too furious and too tired to cry, although we both needed to and my father was just at a loss. We would need more than $200.00 in cash to spring the car. We got the cash from an ATM and cabbed down to the middle of nowhere, by the Hudson River dock.

The pre-dawn air cut like dull razorblades and the dirty signs tacked haphazardly on the grey concrete walls of the prison-like towing office spelled out confusing rules that made us more furious. I moved to go with my father to get the car after he'd paid the ransom, but they wouldn't let me accompany him. He didn't want me standing outside alone in the middle of a dark and cavernous garage, but I assured him I would be fine. We got the car and made it back to Cedar Lane in Teaneck, New Jersey by 5a.m. or soon thereafter.

At 8:30, I had to go back into the city to a day job. My father would go to rehearsal for work on creating a new ballet for The Alvin Ailey American Dance Theater, called *The Winter in Lisbon*, a tribute to the late Dizzy Gillespie that would become to this day one of his most celebrated ballets.

Weight descending

It was during that last ballet, under the pressure of all that was going on with Chip at the time, when my father felt such great incapacitation. When Judith Jamison, the artistic director of The Ailey Company, approached my father to create a piece in tribute to Mr. Gillespie, who happened to be very ill at the time, we were in the midst and at the height of Chip's nervous breakdown. My father was exhausted after those visits; they seemed to drain the very blood from his body. He was so tired. He would say to me, "I'm about to do this ballet in three weeks and I haven't even *listened* to the music." I would reply, "Just take your time. You will when you're ready." The next time he would say, "I've listened to the music, but I can't get a hook into it. It's not giving me any pictures. It's just not happening."

I simply listened, knowing that it was exactly his kind of music. This was part of his era, and the music ordinarily would have made him reel with pictures, feelings, and inspiration. Instead he said, "Holly, I don't think I can do it. I'm tired."

I told him, "You have to do it. This is an important tribute. You'll find it. It will probably be your best work."

He had justifiable reasons not to do the work but he needed to; he needed to save himself. It had been he who had taught me the credo *your work will save you*. He had a hard time in the beginning rehearsal period. He told me his thoughts and worries were elsewhere. He was feeling added pressure to do right by Mr. Gillespie, as well as by the company. "All these eyes are looking to me, and I don't know how I'm getting from one step to the other," he said.

However, after much prayer and emotional teetering, my father did drag himself to the rehearsals day after day to create that tribute to Dizzy Gillespie, who unfortunately passed before the ballet premiered. Perhaps the passing of that great jazz giant brought to mind my father's losses at that particular time when it seemed his whole world was hanging by a thread.

Only two times did I hear my father express a longing for his parents to still be alive to witness what he'd accomplished and created. Moments would creep up on him and he would talk about missing his mother terribly. The first time was during the success of *Bubbling Brown Sugar*, during its run on Broadway. The second time was during the premiere night of *The Winter in Lisbon*.

Though he sometimes experienced feelings of angst sometimes when creating, he would always regain his footing. One step would lead to another and before he knew it, he'd be flying again, and *it*, the thing, would find its way. He said it was larger than he. He always recognized his gifts being given by God and that they were meant to be shared and honored. Ultimately, I believe he trusted himself and the process of creating, though not always without some inner struggle. As I watched him work, I also saw him try to make sense of it all. He was visibly fighting to keep our entire family boat afloat. And at the top of his list, he was trying to make sense of Chip's state and nightmarish journey. He wanted to understand it and fix it. My father's eyes would rest on mine many times throughout those days and plead with me to give him the answer: *Will Chip be okay? Will he survive this? Will we all survive this?*

CHAPTER 11

ANOTHER SHOE DROPS

A T TIMES, WHEN the chemical levels were right, Chip seemed content to be with his new community of friends in the psychiatric building of St. Vincent's. At other times, he pleaded with us to take him home. He was very aware and confused by Parker's lack of visiting. Parker's presence, in general, had become more and more scarce during the period when Chip was admitted. Although Parker had been Chip's confidant and caretaker while in Europe, soon after their return to the States he was often nowhere to be found. Perhaps Parker's decreasing presence had begun shortly after the shocking news that Chip shared with us one day on the phone.

When he was first admitted, he was allowed a phone call. The three of us were all at home and on the phone at the same time taking turns talking to Chip. He began ranting. It was during this manic phone call that Chip blurted out that he and our father were HIV positive. He also told us that they had been knowingly positive for ten years.

I am quite sure that Chip did not pause, even to take a breath. But in our minds, everything stopped as he ceaselessly rambled on. We knew enough to be shocked by what we'd heard, but not enough to feel the full weight of what those three letters implied. It's not a thing you can know. What did

HIV mean exactly? Huge stigmas were still very much attached to the topic of HIV. Our father was horrified, furious, ashamed, and sorry. He didn't want us to find out in that way. We were still his children, after all, and he reserved the right to deal with it on his terms. I never knew just how they contracted it and the how is of no importance to me. I don't need to know. As difficult as that news was, as well as having received it in that way, there was no time for wallowing or blame.

A prelude

Aside from Chip's battle with being bipolar, he also was beginning to show physical symptoms of HIV and would be at the mercy of two protocols at the same time. So many drugs, so little help. It was all taking an emotional toll, both physically and emotionally, on my father.

As usual, here and abroad, my father's work commitments didn't end. After months of shuttling Chip back and forth between St. Vincent's and home, Chip was released with the hope of its being permanent, provided he would take his meds. Our private sentiment was "good luck." My father and I were hopeful, but we honestly did not see that lasting. We brought Chip home that final time and so began his journey with the insidious disease that is full-blown AIDS. For a short while, things were good, but he developed uncontrollable shaking in his hands and legs. Walking became very challenging. He was also wasting away rapidly, painfully thin and frail. As Chip's health worsened, I licked my wounds of a marriage recently failed and decided to stay in the States.

I got my own apartment on the Lower East Side. I was resolved to pick up the pieces of my life. After a few last gigs as a dancer in New York, culminating with the Essence Awards choreographed by Michael Peters (who choreographed Michael Jackson's "Thriller," "Beat It," and many others) I focused on acting again. But time had marched on and I was four years older. I was no longer the only biracial female with a full head of corkscrew curls. It also seemed that every actor I'd known, of every ilk, had all gotten on that same plane to California; the one that I put on the back burner for Europe. I booked some acting work that didn't pay well. My heart wasn't in it. I gradually began to turn to writing. I now had solitary time to think about my life. I was again a single woman living in Manhattan.

My father was still dealing with Chip, and the struggle was hard for him, especially without me there on a regular basis. Parker would make sporadic appearances. I didn't like going to the house anymore because Chip had become so bitter. His critical comments and disappointments were just waiting for me to arrive. I would visit the house to see my father, but seeing Chip was becoming increasingly more challenging. I was also starting to resent the obvious toll that all of Chip's issues were taking on my father. I would make excuses not to go out to the house and excuses to leave soon, once there.

Chip had drained so much of our family's life's blood that we were emotionally bankrupt from it all. We'd lost our ability to laugh and rise above our situation with our usual sardonic humor. It had been too hard for too long. Some kind of irreparable shift had occurred, and it wasn't over yet. For Parker and me, the battleground had just been laid. There was much more to come that would change our lives forever. If I thought a blow had been dealt when Chip's illnesses had begun, it was merely a precursor of what we were about to go through. Our father was losing ground. It was imperceptible to me, but it was happening. The truth was, I didn't want to see it.

Holiday shock

I talked to Parker one day on the phone and he said something about our father having fainted. I had been coming to the house less and less, and knew that my father was upset with me because of this. I felt he was being a bit dramatic in an effort to woo me back to the fold. I knew that he was desperate to escape but couldn't. There was a day when Chip called me at my pay-the-rent retail job, ranting and raving about my lack of concern. He actually called me a bitch. He told me that my father was not well and that all I cared about was myself. I didn't pay him much mind, though I definitely did not appreciate being called a bitch by him or anyone else, manic or not. I knew that if my father really wasn't feeling well, he would reach out to me.

In the meantime, I encouraged him to take a little trip away from it all by himself. He was thinking about going to an island somewhere, but kept second-guessing the decision. I couldn't understand why he was so unsure. To me, there seemed no better time to help him to restore what had been so broken, physically and emotionally. Not long before, he had mounted an updated version of *Bubbling Brown Sugar* in Amsterdam. He was beyond exhaustion and desperately needed a rest. I said, "Go!" It was nearing the holidays. He had persuaded our old devoted housekeeper, Dora, to stay with Chip while he was away. Upon hearing that news, I began to relax a bit, especially knowing that with Dora at the house there would be little worry. When my father boarded a plane for Aruba, I exhaled a sigh of relief. I thought to myself, *now things will be better.*

It turned out that while in Aruba, he fainted on the beach and with a lot of help from the airline, was on his way back home. He went straight from the plane to Emergency at St. Vincent's. He called my brother to tell him he was en route to the hospital and didn't tell me. This was a deliberate move on his part, to let me know that he was very angry with me for not taking him seriously. I was hurt. It was always I he had come to for solace and support. No matter. I got over myself and raced to join Parker at Emergency. My father wouldn't even look me in the eyes at first. Upon seeing him, I was in utter shock. What had happened? Overnight he seemed to have become this frail man in a wheelchair who could barely keep his head up. I didn't recognize him. He looked to be about ninety years old. He was diminutive, emaciated and bewildered. I heard the sound of something breaking, like delicate china, and realized it was my heart.

While Parker and I got our father settled in the hospital, our home away from home, Chip was almost a prisoner of the upstairs floor in the house because neuropathy had taken his legs. He was, by that time, almost completely immobile from the waist down. When he wanted to come downstairs, he would slide down the way we used to do as kids. When he'd lost the will and the strength to slide, he had to be carried down. During this time, he was mostly disoriented and very drugged. Thank God my brother had recently emerged to be there for all of Chip's physical needs and was strong enough to get him downstairs. He could no longer clean himself or feed himself. The meds were ravaging his vital organs. He was often impacted due to the disease, and Parker wasn't squeamish about doing whatever was necessary because he loved Chip.

Chip's appetite had gone and visiting upstairs was like walking into a small warehouse stocked with empty cans of Ensure—the only thing he could keep down. The space started to look like something reminiscent of how little Edie and her mother existed in *Grey Gardens*. Well, maybe not that bad, but the demands were overwhelming. Parker was now the primary caretaker, with Dora needing to return to her own family. I was essentially dealing with my father in New York, while my brother held down the fort in Jersey.

Once again, Chip needed the care of the hospital and we admitted him for the last time. Now he and my father were in the same hospital but on different floors. At times, it was like playing musical hospital rooms, but instead of music to accompany our mad dashes from floor to floor, we had the steady hum of the yellow flickering lights overhead. Some days were spent simply running from one room to the other, to bring them this or straighten out that. In lucid moments, they would send notes to one another, making the other bust out laughing. They also constantly called one another on their room phones. I don't know if their being separated made things better or worse. I do recall that my father elected to remain apart from Chip during that time. Seeing Chip at that stage, as they battled, was too cruel a thing to witness up close. He knew Chip was failing fast and he preferred to remember him in all his glory. One also must remember the vanity of both these men. They would both go out *with bells on*, heads held high, a quick quip, and a last check in the mirror.

Tender mercies

The other thing that was happening was the start of a sweet friendship that would turn into the love of my life. It was Maurice Hines who brought Byron Stripling and me together. Byron had seen me dance the tango in *Harlem Suite* and I'd heard about his heavy-hitting trumpet chops from many in the business. Maurice brought us together at a well-known "gypsy"—Broadway dancers—party thrown by performer Jeffrey Thompson. We met at a time when I needed a friend more than I realized. For six months he was simply my best friend before anything romantic began. He would pick me up at the hospital in the evenings and take me out for a bite to eat. He did this consistently through Chip's and my father's illness. He waited so patiently during a very difficult time. He asked for nothing in return, and I looked forward to his quiet company. When he went on tour to Europe or Japan, I realized how much I missed him, and bit by bit the missing turned to longing and the longing turned to love. Without being in search of it, I'd fallen crazy in love with the man.

Byron has always protected the precious and fragile gem of my heart and loved me unconditionally. He has seen me through all my many storms, and time after time led me safely to shore. He is a wonderful father and he's crazy about our children and me. He knows that to this day, especially when his 6' 3" frame is wearing a tux, I am instantly weak at the knees, and the honest truth is that he's stuck with me. He has had countless reasons not to stay when things got tough, but he never left. Interestingly, it has been the men in my life who have been my heroes. It has been my father, Chip, Chi-chi, Lorenzo James, as well as those I've been involved with over the years who have consistently and effortlessly *had my back.* And at the top of that list is Byron. He is my best and most cherished friend. I believe my father's spirit was instrumental in making this angel stay.

The first farewell

I remember the last time I saw Chip. I went to his room, high up in the hospital building and stared with unspeakable sadness at what had become of the man I once had wanted *out* of my life. Those harsh memories came flooding back. Then all at once they were replaced with my happy recollections of laughter, joking, our friendship, and the love we allowed to take us to the end of our journey together. He lay there unmoving in his mask of AIDS. He was hooked to wires that monitored his vitals, his mouth was caked with the bright orange salve the nurses continuously swabbed on his lips to help keep them from cracking, his feet and hands had blown up to ridiculous size, and there was the peach fuzz of hair. He wasn't there—not the Chip we'd known. What was left was a shell, an encasement, a coffer, a vessel, and that was all. His song had left his body. His spirit had flown away.

Chip died on February 14, 1994. Soon after his death, my father returned home from the hospital and was feeling relatively good, all things considered. I think Chip's death had given him a renewed determination to fight even harder to stay alive. He wasn't ready to be swept away just yet. He gathered his courage and was determined to win. On the evening of Chip's funeral, Dad, Parker, and I were all there in our father's bedroom and silent. Like my favorite black-and-white photo, we'd arrived back to the three of us once again. Parker and I were about to leave for the service at the Methodist church. I remember the lights being so bright in my father's bedroom. It seemed overwhelmingly lit up. I think it was early evening, but already dark on that day in February. My father sat straight up looking like the dancer he was, ready at the barre for the lesson to begin, neat as always in his pressed sheets with his glasses on.

"Are you sure you don't want to go?" I asked.

"No," he replied. "I just can't, Holly." We left. It was a very simple and lovely service. There were theater friends, our dear family friend Lorenzo James, and Chip's sister, Kim. There were a few surprises, including the record producer Dick Scott. I had written a poem for Chip that I recited and barely got through it. Everyone's prayers were sincere and the energy was peaceful. Parker and I returned home sharing happy reminiscences and heavy hearts.

I miss him now more and more. I miss the way he made sure we had enough winter clothes on and that we always had more than enough to eat. I miss his big laugh and his big hands, his beautiful, wide, toothy smile, and the way his eyes got wet and glassy for no reason at all. I miss him for being careful and nervous about all the things parents are meant to be careful and nervous about. I miss how he guzzled champagne and stashed pints of Häagen Dazs butter pecan ice cream under his bed. I miss the 6'2" man who believed in fairy tales. His dreams had so nearly come true. He did, after all, get his family, as imperfect as we all were.

It wasn't until I was in college that things between Chip and me finally began to change for the better. I finally began to understand how he might have felt those years when I wouldn't accept him. It was later, when I'd moved to Holland, that I grew to love and appreciate him on a deeper level. When I'd gotten married for the first time, Chip showed me an incredibly supportive side, despite my father's feelings about it. He, too, was not fully supporting the marriage, but he continued to talk to me about it. At that time, it was Chip's ear that I confided in. He gave me space for making my own decisions even if it would end up proving to be a mistake. It would be my mistake.

Little did I realize that for years he'd been trying to find a place in my corner and understood the hurt that my brother and I were going through. I had to catch up. He often had experienced firsthand the manipulations and bitterness displayed by my mother during those early years. Thankfully, he valued and believed in the future that he and my father could share, and accepted the terms that came along with loving my father *and* his children. The two were non-negotiable. He did love us like his own, unconditionally, and tried his damndest to make us feel safe and important. His efforts were inexhaustible and he never ... left. He didn't abandon ship, didn't run away or say *to hell with it!* I know there were many times when he felt that way, and with good reason, but clearly he was capable of withstanding all the pressures. Luckily for us, he stayed.

That is the true testament of who Chip was and not my Faustian-like perception of who I'd made him out to be. He was not my enemy. I finally began trusting Chip. In letting down my guard I became less self-absorbed and was able to see him for all that was positive and good. I was also allowing more space for human beings to be imperfect and more human. It took years to give into the love between Chip and me. I believe that my love for him was always there. I just didn't know what to do with it because my own sadness and anger blurred my vision. However, despite the many years during most of my growing up when I did not accept him, the memories today remain endearing and beloved. What I like to remember now is the laughter and the theater we had in our lives.

As a child, my recollection of first meeting Chip was confined to a general description of a visitor. Now, as an adult, that first meeting would be more generous. The scene was dark or dimly lit, in shadows. Chip was a tall, impressive visitor, statuesque, and red-brown in color. At the ends of his long arms were massive hands and endlessly slender fingers. His eyes were almond-shaped, set deep, and wide. They looked as though outlined in coal. My cousin Malik has eyes like that. They are stunning and smoky. Getting lost in them makes you share in a silent telling of ancient Egyptian tales. The eyes possess a dark border, an emphasis, an Arabian secret, naturally and without effort. Chip's lips were rounded mounds of mocha chocolate truffles shaped into a mouth without sharp lines that rested within a face often pleading and sad. That beautifully full mouth opened up to a rich voice of dim forests and formidable oceans. There was majesty there. It came from deep within his rippling diaphragm. When it reached the lips, it escaped to produce a mesmerizing effect and left you drunk, wanting to curl up inside his voice and stay. And when he sang, it was like velvet that wrapped around each song, each tone, and every note.

With each day of missing him more, I appreciate with newness another piece of Chip Walter Garnett. He was, above all things, another human being among us who wanted nothing more than to be acknowledged for the talents he possessed and loved for who he was.

CHAPTER 12

NEW JOURNEY

WHEN DID IT change? When did the shift happen from a world consumed with Chip's caretaking to that of my father's? Probably news of his fainting spells was the first real indication of something very wrong about to break the surface. It's true that I wouldn't allow myself to believe the same demise was capable of befalling my father. Then came his solo trip to Aruba that culminated in an emergency flight home and the beginning of a very rapid end. When his decline started, it felt like living in an endless bad dream of long days and interminable nights. And in between, we waited for the results of the never-ending tests.

On that first visit to St. Vincent's from his Aruba trip, he went immediately into quarantine because of the fear that he had contracted TB. No one was allowed to enter his room without donning a salmon-colored paper mask to cover the nose and mouth. I would see him, before entering, through the small window of the cell-like room that kept him there. The quarantine room was different from the regular hospital rooms, which in comparison had started to look like a suite at the Sherry-Netherland. He would sit waiting for me—terrified. It was like something out of *The Hot Zone,* but without the standard CDC white garb and space helmet. It seemed we'd stepped into one of those movie thrillers we looked forward to watching together on the weekends with our afghans and BLTs. Thankfully, he didn't spend much time there, as it was discovered he did not have TB.

The days, weeks, and months that followed were as incomprehensible as they were unmercifully real. It was a constant steadiness of admittance and release from the much too familiar St. V's Hospital. My father's prognosis ebbed and flowed. It was another roller coaster of ups and downs, elations and deflations, numbers hopeful and numbers not, viral load heavy and light as he slid between being detectable and undetectable. Though we woke up with his reality every day, I was functioning primarily in a state of denial. However, until the inevitable arrived, we were in the fight for his life *by any means necessary*. Day by day we found a ritual groove of getting through minute by minute, resolved to stay positive and win. There was a moment in the eye of this hurricane when I came close to buckling under the weight of it all.

We had come from one of my father's regular check-ups at Dr. Bellman's for all the various blood work and regulatory meds. He would need to be on a daily drip at home, three times a day, of Acyclovir and Epogen. I would need to administer this drip for him, instructed by a nurse who came to the house to show me how. I dreaded that day and resented the life and death responsibility.

I didn't want to do it. I didn't want to be the one responsible to remember to clean the catheter sufficiently, to inject the right fluid at the right time, and to make sure the air bubbles were released—the way we've all seen on TV daytime dramas thinking it's a BS acting choice. It isn't an acting choice; it's real and I was scared to death to add this to my list of tasks. When the nurse came, I had to excuse myself a couple of times to take a deep breath and wipe away the wet that would not cease from welling up in my eyes. While I was trying to pull myself together in another room, I could overhear my father whispering to her that I would be all right, but "she has to do so much now." A fresh surge of tears found its way back up upon hearing that, and I needed to compose myself yet again. He knew how much I adored him; that's why he didn't trust anyone else to take care of things.

There had been a few times when I needed to be in Manhattan for the day. My brother's girlfriend was living in the house with us and pregnant with Parker's child. She would stay with my father all day, but he refused to eat until I returned.

"Dad, why didn't you *eat* anything?"

"I was waiting for you. I like *your* cooking."

"*Dad.*" I went on to gently reprimand him as though he were five years old, but his words of endearment were sweet to my ears. I was doing something right. He trusted me and liked my company. That sense I felt of having provided him with some comfort filled my heart. Much of the time, I was unsure and going it blindly. I learned to give him his treatments and it became as natural to both of us as brushing our teeth. I learned what to do when the saline burned his veins going in too strong, knew which pill to give him for extra comfort, organized his other ten to twelve pills of the day, and knew what each one was for.

One day, during one of his stints back in the hospital, I'd arrived as usual first thing in the morning to find him completely strung out. He looked like he was on heroin. He could hardly move enough to get out the words to express his confusion at why he was so out of it.

I looked at the drip and flew to the nurse's station in a contained rage. I knew instinctively and immediately what was wrong with him. I had come to know everyone on rotation for my father during the day. I knew them by name, and they were all fantastic, but I didn't know the night staff. I found the head nurse, who was a very compassionate and intelligent man. I asked him to please look at what my father had been given during the night, as there was no reason why he should have been in the state I found him in. He was a different person the day before, when he had been alert and feeling pretty good. The nurse went into my father's room and agreed that something was wrong. Upon further investigation, we learned to the utter shock and dismay of the head nurse and me that my father had been given double the dosage of what he was supposed to have gotten. My whole body went slack with sheer disbelief, horror, and gratefulness that they hadn't overdosed him quite literally to death. I remember having an epiphany at that moment. I became acutely aware of how important my piece of this insane puzzle fit into helping to keep my father alive.

My thoughts landed on a line from *Mommie Dearest* and the famous, "I'm not mad at you, I'm mad at the dirt" scene. In that moment, Joan Crawford also mutters, "You've got to stay on top of it *every minute*!" I understood that line then with renewed clarity. When circumstance forces one to be at the mercy of the hospitals, it is absolutely essential to become intimately involved with all that goes on and all that is administered. I was there, thank God, to oversee everything that had to do with my father's care. I had caught what happened because I was on top of it every minute. It also made me think about all the patients on that floor battling AIDS who didn't have that some-body who had their back, to protect their integrity, and watch their meds like a hawk.

There were many moments during Chip's and my father's stay at the hospital that gave me pause to reflect on the state of support and loving care seeming to elude many of the patients on Cronin 7, let alone in these United States of America and around the globe. For the first time, I witnessed the reality of the terrible loneliness that often accompanied so many on this floor who were battling AIDS and fighting daily for their lives. There were a few of these souls I got to know just a little bit. Although their approach to life armed them with the ability to laugh in face of devastation, they were often going it alone. While my father found himself turning down the steady stream of those wishing to visit him in the hospital, there were those who longed for their family to finally spend a little time by their side and embrace them at death's door.

Lucky ones

I recall one man in particular who pulled at my heartstrings for want of companionship and a little attention. At one point he and my father spent time in the same room. He looked to be about 90 pounds soaking wet, as did most of the patients on that floor, including my father. This thirty-something young man had a shock of blondish-orange hair that made him look like a frail and kooky kind of bird. His manner was sweet, sad, and impish. It seemed as though his constitution and whole body might blow into dust if someone so much as looked at him with the slightest judgment or reproach. His cheeks hung with that all-too-familiar pull of gravity that one recog-nized bed after bed. The I.V. was stuck into one of his last available veins and was attached to the fluid suspended like a last chance in the air.

We talked. He would pause to catch a few missed breaths. His spirit was kind and easy. We would all laugh together. My father liked his company and found his sweetness endearing. I would catch him watching us with bitter sweetness and obvious envy. Once he even mentioned the loneliness at not having a warm and loving family to visit him. I believe my daily stays left him speechless. I asked him about his visitors, although I don't recall so much as one. I remember him sighing often. It was true. He told me he had no visitors. His family had disowned him when he came out. It wasn't possible for them to accept his homosexuality, let alone the knowledge of his having contracted AIDS. His lover had also bailed.

How is that possible, I wondered? How do human beings do this to one another? As he continued to talk, it was as if it were the absence of these players in his life that were sucking his life's breath and not something called AIDS. It was their lack of love that was also draining his precious moments. I didn't know what to say. It was comfort that he yearned for and a few moments of human contact and reassurance. Someone to say, "It's gonna be all right. I'm here, it's gonna be all right." There are times during caretaking when little white lies are told in the name of keeping up the spirit and defending hope. This is sometimes true even within the most honest of relationships. A time also comes when simply *being* and sharing the moments with the ones you care about is enough. Listening to my sweet friend, I wished that something might change for him before it was too late. The man in the bed next to my father had no one.

As the seriousness of Dad's growing illness became more real, I was beginning to appreciate the necessity that his journey be one filled with peace in his heart and overflowing with love surrounding him. I felt it was my responsibility to ensure that this happen. After all, I was there. He had someone. He had me, he had Lorenzo, he had Parker, and all the many who cared and loved him intensely. I felt that my father's comrade deserved not only an apology from those in his immediate existence, but also on behalf of humanity. His loneliness embarrassed me. The most I felt I could do at that time was to offer getting him something on my frequent outings on my father's behalf. Upon occasion, he would shyly ask if I might pick him up a chocolate bar. When I returned and presented him with the small token, he rejoiced as if he'd witnessed the most astonishing offering. His delight gave me great pleasure and that seemingly small pleasure appeared to sometimes make his day.

One morning I arrived to spend my day with my father, at the usual 7 a.m., to find our friend's bed empty. He had gone home—not yet in the metaphoric sense—and we had no idea who would be his caretaker, but the two of us wished him well. We would miss his gentle soul. To myself, I silently and genuinely hoped to never see him again, unless he was walking down the street spry and full of health.

The cliché is true. When you lie on your deathbed or face the inevitability of a loved one's passing on, it isn't material things that are at the top of the list. It is the effect of other lives and loves in our life. They are the comforts. It has not been my own preparation for death that has led me to this conclusion. It has been the experience of bearing witness, many times over, to those endearing people in my life who have been lost to AIDS. They were the ones who taught me as they traveled on.

Always waiting

When my father became ill, he and I were completely dependent upon Parker for our transportation to the city for all the crucial doctor appointments. However, the first challenge was to actually connect with Parker, despite his having three beepers and no job at which to contact him. When we needed him most, he was tougher to get in contact with than a pop icon. He'd traded in his nine-to-five for mysterious street hustles and had the added luxury of my father's partial financial support. He was living the life of Riley on borrowed time.

Time after time, while our father stood with shaky legs looking as dapper as possible, we would spend his already nervous time waiting and waiting and waiting for Parker to arrive. Those visits to the very special Paul C. Bellman, M.D.—dubbed the "pope of Greenwich Village," were excruciating days for my father. Before the HIV, his greatest anxiety had been getting his blood pressure checked; it ran high in the Wilson family and was something he always had to keep an eye on. The stress he felt when having to make the appointments with Dr. Bellman loomed for days and weeks in angst of what the many results might prove. He'd probably longed for the days when all he had to worry about was his blood pressure. Going to the doctor for AIDS-related check-ups involved lots of blood work, endless checks for this and that, as well as the dreaded number results for his T-cell count and viral load. On the days preceding one of these visits, he would be terrified. Yet there he'd be, after stumbling while getting dressed, forcing himself to eat the tiniest morsel, taking his fifty million meds (blue ones, pink ones, red ones, white ones), enduring his daily drip, and steadying himself to look composed while waiting for Parker to pick us up.

As the minutes and half-hours passed, he would grow understandably more and more anxious. The trembling in his hands would become more pronounced, and I would become more and more angry. By the time Parker would finally breeze in and get my father to his appointment, late, as usual, Dad's composure and confidence were completely shattered. His legs would be like rubber and his eyes were wide with fear as we made our way to the doctor.

Parker knew what creating such a situation did to our father. He knew that it took everything he had just to get pants on, button a shirt, and put on socks. These things my father tried his damndest to do on his own because he had such pride. Parker knew that, more than anything, those doctor visits played havoc with our father's thoughts and worries about what awaited him. He knew it all too well because he had been Chip's caretaker when our father started to become ill. Perhaps he just couldn't take it anymore and didn't want to be there 24/7 to witness my father's unraveling. Whatever his reasons, he continued to make us wait as we tracked him down during some of our greatest hours of need. Thank God I had Byron by my side to help soften the many blows and challenges.

Byron met my father for the first time in the lobby of St. Vincent's. Byron and I met my father and Lorenzo there after he'd been to see his doctor for a check-up. What Byron recalls is this man, obviously exhausted and struggling to keep it together but maintaining his dignity with ferocity. He immediately embraced my father. It was a beautiful instinct, and we all spent a little time together. Some years later, Lorenzo shared with me that my father strongly approved of Byron and liked him very much. Through Lorenzo, I had my father's blessing. He knew that with Byron in my corner, I would be all right. He was right. *Still* right.

Damned legs!

During the journey I took alongside my father, it seemed at times the symptoms were invisible to me. His increasing thinness was something that perhaps I'd grown accustomed to. The darkening of his skin, especially in the face and hands, were also symptoms I'd come to expect and was all too familiar with. Nonetheless, it was one of the things that he most loathed about how the disease was cruelly eating away at his body. It attacked his vanity for the entire world to see. Those universal symptoms made him a marked man. He'd say, "And this damned Bactrim!" When the medicines began to shade his skin in that unnatural way, with its black-brown splotches helping to further hollow out the prominence of his skull, he took to his mirror.

Towards the end of his illness, he was never without his small round army-green-colored mirror. When he sat in his bed, it accompanied him at his bedside table. When he sat on the overstuffed white chair in his bedroom—the chair he'd once commanded but that later came to swallow him whole and made him look as small as a child in dress-up—he lodged the little mirror safely in between the cushion, where he could quickly retrieve it at any time. The mirror, his square wooden hairbrush with the coarse bristles, his Chap Stick, and his Vicks inhaler were all the things he kept within arm's reach. These items helped to keep him psychologically afloat. These were things he could not physically part from while on his raft, and the mere fact that he never lost heart in keeping up appearances was always a comfort to me.

More than damning the medicine called Bactrim, however, was his cursing the growing unsteadiness of his once vital and sure legs. It was very difficult to watch him wobbling like a newborn foal. In the beginning, he still maintained exercises to keep his muscles alive. This was a man who gave himself a ballet barre nearly every day of his life; whether working or on holiday. But even during his stronger periods, once the symptoms had taken hold, his legs never again had the same strength or function. Even despite the legs not being what they were, I would often walk into his hospital room at 7:00 a.m. to find him sitting erect doing arm exercises from his bed. I didn't fully recognize the essentialness of my own legs until I watched my father struggle with his. They were not his own. They were unwieldy and unpredictable. They buckled under his weight and, rubber-like, walked him in the opposite direction, either too fast or too slow. This ultimate lack of control over his body had his otherwise strong will and positive thinking at a loss. When he lost control of his legs, he quickly surrendered to it. When he let it go, a big part of his spirit went with it as well. It was at that point that the disease chalked a big one up for the home team. It was winning.

One of the most difficult letters he had to compose was to the Dutch producers in Amsterdam to inform them that he would need to renege on their agreement for him to begin work on creating an original musical production. He dictated the letter to me, as his once-beautiful handwriting had become too shaky to decipher. We sat outside the house on Cedar Lane. It was a warm, clear, blue spring day. The magnolia tree on our lawn was blowing its pink petals to scatter and dance all around us like a light, happy tornado. I knew this moment had to come. For some time he talked about needing to be ready for that production. "I've gotta get these legs together, Holly." It was getting closer to the audition time, but I wanted to let him come to the reality of what was inevitable on his own. I trusted he would come to it. Hell, even I still believed he would rally back to do the work.

I sent that damned letter to the Dutch producers, knowing how it killed him to have to bow out. The work, his work, was always so important to him. It had always been the thing to keep him going when other pieces of his life became seemingly insurmountable. Over and over again his work had been his savior. And then all at once, the inability to do the thing he loved seemed the barometer or indication of his life being over.

I silently and respectfully observed as his more private demons began to reveal themselves to me. The illness rendered him increasingly more vulnerable and I had become old enough to understand more. I knew that his guilt over some great events in his life made him feel blaringly imperfect. The most significant of those was his guilt about our mother's absence from our lives. He endlessly felt the need to overcompensate for this incomprehensible circumstance. He felt somehow responsible.

I also know that the emotional fallout from his infidelities affected him as well. We never spoke openly about all of it, but a name here or there would be divulged and he would reminisce with a nostalgic devotion. At times a name was accompanied by a subtle acknowledgment of those choices he perhaps wished he hadn't made. Still and all, selfish or not, he never fully apologized for his romantic choices or his lifestyle choices. He was very sorry for things not working out for *us* with our mother in the way he had hoped. However, he would also not fall into the trap of taking full blame for that great disappointment. Instead, despite his anger regarding my mother, he continued to always hang a lovely photo of her on the wall, dancing among all the others who held a special place in his heart. His philosophy rested with the *good* memories and with the fact that she would forever be the mother of his children, and that he celebrated.

After the letter was written and sent, it was the last time he spent in that house. His next trip to St. Vincent's would be his last. Once again, he was seemingly getting better and then he'd gotten worse. Back to the hospital we went.

The vision

A new head of this insidious disease reared itself, ever so subtly. During the course of his hospital stays, Dad was moved several times from room to room for different reasons. In this last hospital room, directly across from his bed, was a framed poster. The poster was of a winding road that led, at the bottom, to a youngish man. The man stood facing out at the onlooker. The poster was colorful, with bright purples, blues, yellows, greens, and reds. The young man who stood at the beginning of this path was not very significant-looking. He was one-dimensional with bland features and "flat," but with a slow smile on his face. His hands were by his side, with palms facing out. One day, my father said to Parker and me that he'd noticed the young man in the poster moving.

"Moving?"

"He moves his hands." He showed us what he meant by demonstrating with his hand and bony fingers dark brown and splotchy from Bactrim. It was like a movement of beckoning someone, but turned upside-down, similar to the slow fanning of a Daddy Longlegs; one finger after the other. He then began turning his wrist slightly, as if gently stirring warm water clockwise. It was a specific and hypnotic movement. At first the poster intrigued him; later it disturbed him. The movement grew. What had begun at the start of the week as a simple isolated gesture had become by the end of the week a traveling figure. The young man soon started walking. He saw him walking up the path. Each day the picture had become a more complicated issue. The figure became more active and more agitating to him until finally he had me cover the poster completely with a hospital bed sheet.

This was the first of several hallucinations he would experience. Like Chip, he also became constantly distracted and preoccupied with numbers. I believe that the traveling figure in the frame was a hallucination, as opposed to a vision. The vision that occurred later was a thing I would feel in the very marrow of my mortality and a precursor to the devastating inevitability of his. I've heard it said that for the person who is at the door and ready, death is like a welcome lover and the surrender an ultimate peace.

It was a sunny morning, as were most during my father's last early July mornings. I usually arrived at 7 a.m. at Cronin 7. Sunshine was flooding the hallways, and the mood was peaceful. The hectic hustle and bustle had not yet begun. In the later stage of my father's illness, he spent a lot of time staring out the window or into the space around him. What appeared to be nothingness and air to me was often clear, real, and lively for him. There was no doubt that the hallucinations were very much a part of his every day. Who knew how much was real, imagined, dementia, or drug induced? How much was the experience of his nearing homecoming?

On this particular day, it was the closest I'd come to sharing his sacred and mysterious journey near its end.

"Hi, Dad," I said, as I gave him a kiss on his forehead. He was sitting up as straight as a reed in his chair. I sat down near him on the end of his bed. Usually I found him in bed, and as the morning wore on, he eventually would make his way to the chair. That is what constituted his exercise, moving from bed to chair. This from a man who'd lived his life dancing through space. There wasn't much walking at all anymore.

Did he smile that morning when I kissed him? He was completely distracted. "Distracted" is not right. He was not being torn from one thing to another. He was fully absorbed. He felt my presence, but had his mind and his eyes on something important. He was transported, or perhaps it was the beginning stage of his being transported. I watched him, sat with him, and tried to be as still as the shards of light strewn on the cold, grey, hard floor of that room. I was trying to follow his lead. Something other was happening. It made me uneasy and jumpy inside my skin, although the moment was calm. It was, in fact, one of the more beautiful days in his room, with the flowers sitting on the sill because he always wanted and needed them around him.

"Are you okay, Dad?" He nodded slowly, deliberately. He was as if in some somber trance. His skin had taken on a yellowish glow and hung in layers on his prominent cheekbones, elbows and knees. What had happened to my strong, invincible father? Over and over again these questions consumed my thoughts, as I tried to strike a bargain with the Almighty.

I kept thinking there must have been some mistake. Surely this could not be happening to my father. But of course, it was happening and had in fact been happening over the course of ten years—lying in wait for just the right amount of stress or other critically negative component to reveal itself. Its wrath was speeding up. We sat together, undisturbed by any administering hospital whatevers. No nurses checked, probed, or stuck anything anywhere. We looked into the sun. Something or someone was there for him, in that sun. What was he seeing? I tried hard to stare into his world but saw only the day: life.

"I see him." He spoke softly because he had so little strength, but he was still speaking then.

"Who, Dad? Who do you see?"

"Charon." I knew who he was talking about.

"The man on the boat." He paused. "The man. He's in the boat. He's waiting for me."

His voice trailed off. There were many long pauses as he told me what he was seeing. It felt as if he and I were moving between two worlds. He was nearly "there," as he described the scene to me and then returned to the sunshine of the day during the pauses in between. It seemed that he was in a darker world. What had given me such a dark picture? Something gave me the impression of muted murkiness. I clearly got a picture of the underworld, as opposed to angels floating amid billowing clouds and blinding brightness. He may have told me the man in the boat was wearing a black hat. If he thought the hat was "sharp" or chic, he would have taken that as a welcoming sign.

"Are you going with him, Dad?"

At that moment, he replied in true Billy fashion. For the briefest moment, his humor was intact. His eyebrows rose slightly as he answered without giving it all away. He was still lucid enough to mess with me a little.

"Maybe."

This meant, "Maybe I will and maybe I won't." It will be whatever it's going to be, and we probably won't know until we get there. He saw what he saw, and I had no doubt it was real for him. It was real for me. And the fact that he'd said "maybe" and not "yes" somehow made it all the more real. The reality of his consideration and unresolved decision made the inevitable as real as sitting on that hospital bed next to my dying father. At the same time, his indecision bought time: perhaps later, perhaps next month, perhaps tomorrow.

"Are you afraid of him, Dad?"

"No." That was all—and all that I could stand.

When that last word was said, in all its finality, the clarity of what was happening and what would happen, ran up into my throat and choked me. I could hardly get out the words to tell him I needed to go and would be right back.

On that day a part of me died as well, and this before his death actually occurred. Another bit of my heart had irreparably cracked and broken. He was telling me he was going. How wonderful that I had been there for him. I was there to witness a prelude to his bodily departure. However, I simply could not breathe in that peaceful sun-filled room. It was one of the few times I could not support my own personal pain of being infuriatingly human, for being utterly helpless and so, so sad. How would I survive the world without him, and more to the point, I didn't want to. Somehow the last breath I took when he finished telling me about Charon got me miraculously to the elevator and down to the main floor.

I held in my whole life—past, present, and future—until, as I walked out of the crowded elevator, Lorenzo James was walking in. I saw only him. I looked into his eyes for help and nearly fell into his arms. My heart exploded somewhere in between his chest and shoulder. It was the place I'd go to on my father when I felt lost and scared. I tried to tell Lorenzo, through tears, what my father had told me. I released the first truckload of grief onto Lorenzo's strong and willing shoulders.

Lorenzo James had been and continues to be one of the truest living angels I have had the blessing of having in my life. He is a man of much mystery and privacy, but his expansive capacity for *giving* is without any veil or pretense. I know that he had been an important friend and confidant to Montgomery Clift and at another time managed the jazz composer Mary Lou Williams. I knew him from his days at The Dance Theatre of Harlem as Arthur Mitchell's right hand, confidant, and friend. When I was younger, I was afraid of him because his looks are arresting and powerful. However, to get to know this man, as I grew older, has been one of the great treasures of my life. I don't think I've ever met anyone as selfless or as tireless when it comes to helping others. He took care of both Chip and my father while they were in the hospital. He would steal into their rooms at odd hours of the day or night to wash their feet, massage their atrophied muscles or give them a shave. I *know* that this man is a living angel among us, and I will be forever grateful for all the love he has showered unconditionally on my family. As I stumbled on, he led me by the elbow, as he always has, to the outside steps of St. Vincent's. There he left me quietly to myself amid the busy regular bright day on 7th Avenue to attempt to somehow make sense of this life. It was the first day I chose not to go back to the hospital to see my father.

CHAPTER 13

THE UNIMAGINABLE

WEEKS LATER, I was in my apartment with my friend Cynthia and Byron. It was around 10:00 p.m. I had been to the hospital earlier and had left and returned a few times throughout the day, never staying for long periods at a time. Towards the end of my father's illness, it was getting harder to bear. He was leaving us, had been leaving us slowly. The phone in the apartment rang. It was August 14. Parker said, "Daddy just went. Daddy just died. I was there. I was with him."

I thought to myself, how fitting. I was glad that he had departed with his son there to set him on his journey. It gave me a certain peace. We'd all had so many ups and downs, so much stress and loss. Regardless to all of it, at the end of the day, the thing that should have meant the most did. At times I hated my brother and at other times I loved him crazy, but I always loved him more. I don't remember much else except that somehow Byron and I arrived at the hospital. We had all been waiting in our own agony for his release, but he kept hanging on. No one thought he would hold on for three weeks past the time the doctors expected. We were readying ourselves. *He* wasn't ready. From all those years of dancing, his heart just didn't give in until that evening.

I remember walking into that hospital, just as I had for the past year, yet that night it was almost as if for the first time. It was as though my mind were taking snapshots of every wall, inch of floor, color, smell and temperature of that night. I recall my calm and my deliberate steps. As everything was speeding in my mind, it was like being in that dream where I feel I'm on a conveyer belt going nowhere: a hamster on a wheel in slow motion. The reality of that finality and fate had finally come to pass. It had arrived and the thoughts that pulled me to his room were simultaneously past and present.

The business that I would have to take care of was soon upon me. That was the part that kept me ticking and that held me together—for the moment. The other part was the treadmill or dread mill. I wanted to run like hell away from that hospital and from people and from life itself. Instead, I kept walking with cinder blocks in my shoes and weights around my ankles. I kept on deliberately and with Byron's hand to help steady me.

My thoughts went to my brother, in the florescent dimly lit room, at the time of his father's last breath. The elevator with the putrid glow and metal handrail I held onto felt as though ascending *up* into quicksand. Lorenzo was already there with Parker. I went in with Byron and then was left alone with my father. I don't think I said anything. I was just quietly staring at his stiffened body and then left to stand in the hallway. Arthur Mitchell was also there. It was just the five of us. We all just stood in the hall, silent. Then Mr. Mitchell said, "You should write his biography."

I replied simply, "I will."

Billy was gone. My father had traveled on but I had been there, by his side, for the whole journey. There was never a moment, a question, a thought, or hesitation about it. He was my father and I loved him madly. I was blessed to have had him in my life and be his doting daughter. He will always be my first knight in shining armor. I look back on all that was so painfully hard during those long months, and it still haunts my heart to recall it. I also look back and remember laughter, always the laughter and the irreplaceable bond we were so fortunate to have shared between us.

Tornado list

The events immediately following my father's death are foggy. So much needed attention and the decision-making felt endless. Although there is much that I don't remember, I do recall sitting in a cramped phone booth near the downstairs cafeteria of St. Vincent's talking with my eyes closed to my guardian angel Aunt Yvonne. My husband always talks on the phone with his eyes closed. I'd never seen anyone do that before. He tells me it helps him to concentrate on what the other person is saying. When I dialed Aunt Yvonne's number to tell her that Billy had passed and heard her voice on the other end, I closed my eyes. I did it to quell the overwhelm of all the many tasks—surreal tasks that swirled just above my head.

There was hospital paperwork, getting in touch with the funeral home that was waiting for my call, contacting the rest of my family, and the most rattling concept of getting his body to Philadelphia to be buried with the family. Lorraine Graves, former ballet mistress of The Dance Theatre of Harlem and another mother-like guardian angel, was incredible. She helped me to find and make arrangements with the funeral home, as her family had been in that very business for years. Aunt Yvonne helped me with everything else, and I don't honestly think I could have gotten through the emotional whirlwind without her constant support from Philadelphia. First and foremost was the burial and transporting my father's beautiful body. Of all the many hours, days, weeks, and even months following his death, I don't remember much. However, the day we all took the trip to Philly to bury our beloved Billy Wilson is a day I will never forget.

Stormy weather

Byron, Lorenzo James, Maurice Hines, and I were catching the train to Philadelphia. My father's casket was traveling in the cargo hold. Along with all of the many emotional preparations and stressful decisions, we were waiting … for Parker. He was late, and the train was on its way. The clock was ticking, and my mind was exploding with grief and anger at this impossible moment of all moments orchestrated by my God-forsaken completely self-absorbed and insensitive fucking brother!

The train began its approach into the station with still no Parker in sight. Lorenzo, forever proactive and clear thinking, had gone ahead and bought a ticket for him so that all he had to do was jump on. As our train was pulling in, here came Parker with his girlfriend and brand-new baby, all panting to make it. If I'd been a man, I probably would have backhanded him across the face—even more insulting than a solid uppercut. All of us were running by that time, out of breath, with various degrees of shock and disbelief as the steel doors slid open for us all to board the Amtrak on Billy's funeral day.

That debacle at Penn Station, at the *beginning* of that day, was for me one of the most upsetting moments to occur. We hadn't even gotten to the damn funeral yet. However, we did all arrive safely and miraculously with our father's precious body in tow. I said nothing to my brother on the ride down or quite possibly for the rest of that day. I was finished with him. After months of chasing him down, begging him to be responsible when we were counting on him most, as he continually broke my father's heart bit by bit with each piece of news from some Southern prison to the infamous New York City "tombs," I was done. Maybe that's why the storm came that day. At the gravesite, a rainstorm that had been gathering momentum all morning became unrelenting. It grew stronger as the funeral wore on. As if on cue or staged by a director of a film crew, the wind whipped the tarp angrily on the earth as the rain came down in cauldrons full: fierce and dramatic. It screamed down as if the dark clouds were grieving. It was pure theater. The heavier the rain and more aggressively the winds blew, the bigger everyone's eyes got as we all looked from one to the other in disbelief and nervous amusement. As the eulogy was spoken, the storm had become so loud that the words were getting lost, then hurled and shouted over the din of rainy fury. Perhaps our father was unhappy with his children for being at odds with one another on his final day of rest. It was always important to him that we understood the necessity to get along and love each other. He drilled into us the importance of being able to depend on the other for strength and support. If our father was angry that day, wherever it was he floated above us, he was very angry. Or he simply wanted to go out with a bang of theater!

The homage

Many angels attended the memorial I organized for my father at St. John the Divine in New York City on October 19, 1994. It is one of the things I am very proud of. For that memorial I brought The Dance Theatre of Harlem and The Alvin Ailey American Dance Theater together on the same stage to perform a selection of work created by my father. Geoffrey Holder's divine presence started everything off by describing Billy "as a man who continued to possess a child-like wonder and curiosity about life." There were also singers to sing from shows he'd choreographed, and a host of lovely speakers, from Judith Jamison to Christopher Sarson, who both spoke eloquently and humorously about their beloved friend. Even those blessed nurses from St. Vincent's Hospital were in attendance, as well as some of the original cast members—once kids but all grown up—from ZOOM! I couldn't have been more touched by such an overwhelming show of affection. It was a beautiful memorial. I know Billy would have been proud. He was, without question, in that gorgeous church with all of us. In fact, his likeness watched over us. The Ailey Company had blown up an enormous photo of my father smiling that sat on an easel upstage throughout the entire memorial. I was on the program to speak that day, but at the last moment, I changed my mind. I had too much to think about, and at the same time I thought of nothing because I was numb. In general, the day was a fog and I needed to grieve.

The grieving room

Trying to put into words what one feels when a loved one dies is as difficult as trying to describe the feeling of falling in love. We ask ourselves questions. What happens when they leave us? Where do they go? Are they all right? Will we see them again? How will we go on without them? And why the hell does everything continue as if nothing has happened?

The grieving process for me hasn't ended, but it keeps changing. Because I had a lot of business to take care of following my father's death, I didn't begin to grieve until a full year later. There is a photo taken of me with my first cousins immediately following my father's funeral. I am glowing, lit up and smiling. We looked as if we were at a party. It was a celebration of sorts, but I was in complete shock. After he died , I knew I needed to hang on until the right time to let it all go. I believe that, like giving birth, grieving is one of the most profoundly individual happenings we can experience in this life. It is based on many variables, but the most overwhelming element seems to be how we relate it to our past, our history and ultimately our childhood.

Our baggage and personal issues come in myriad shapes, sizes, and weight. If one is inclined to allow it, it will all find its way to the surface. That is exactly what lay waiting for me after the smoke had cleared and I exhaled. The journey was as painfully sad as it was gradually healing. Grieving led me to a complete excavation of my life and all that it meant. It seemed I had a frightening amount of work to do on all that I had suppressed and ignored. Feeling it all hit me with such overwhelming force and lack of mercy, I thought I might die. I often felt I could not support the strain of what I was feeling. I began to understand for the first time what heartache and heartbreak meant. I had gotten a taste of it when my first marriage had ended, but this was a horse of different color. It was like a brutal emotional tidal wave that at times would knock me to my knees.

I can recall a moment in particular when Byron was out of town. It was late afternoon and pouring down rain. Grief had pulled me from room to room until I landed in the kitchen. It literally threw me against the bay window, where I clung to it. The windows were like my buoys in the middle of my stormy sea. It was dramatic and theatrical, completely out of my control and real life. I felt like a rag doll as I held onto the frames of those windows and wailed the most primal cries. Sounds came out of me that were anything but familiar, and they scared me. I held onto those windows until I couldn't anymore, and my knees surrendered, bringing me helpless to the wooden floor. Rain was pouring outside. I will never forget that moment. It broke me on that day. Maybe I had the phone in my hand the whole time, or perhaps Byron had called, but I remember sitting utterly defeated and alone in my kitchen and then heard his consoling sweet voice bathe me. I also recall feeling the need to apologize for being a victim to this thing called grief. I'm quite sure I felt I'd lost. It had beaten me. I thought I was stronger than this and I was sorry. I was sorry for bothering Byron, for not being able to move from the floor, sorry for not being able to speak clearly through my sobs, sorry for not being a better daughter, sorry for letting my father die.

"I should have done more! I should have... What should I have done? I didn't think he would die. I just don't understand. It's not fair, it's not fair ... it's not, it's not, not ... fair." Of course, it wasn't fair. Much in life is not fair, but it's part of what we must reconcile within ourselves to somehow accept. Why do we feel responsible and blame ourselves when someone we love passes? Perhaps we need an explanation. There must, after all, be some reason. It's all so surreal and inexplicable.

One of the confusions and resentments that I struggled with was *how was it possible that my father, my protector, my friend, my hero could die before my mother?* It angered me. It was another wrongdoing, another example of cruel irony. I was angry with her and angry with God. It was around this time that my belief in God, in that name, didn't feel as right to me anymore. Plenty of anger to go 'round. Shrapnel still remained from the emotional fallout. And it was all steeped in fear.

There was also a period of time that left me somewhat paralyzed and petrified whenever Byron would walk out of the door. Whether he went to the store or got on a plane, which he did frequently, I feared losing him. I had such anxiety. I would cry sometimes uncontrollably when he left. Grief brought my issues of abandonment to the surface. I was terrified. I felt I could not survive anyone else's leaving. After all, it hadn't been only my father who died but essentially my parents, and that included Chip. He had died six months earlier than my father, to the day, and he had been more a parent to me than my own mother had been.

Death is so humbling. Hopefully it is. For some, it still doesn't drive home in a way that is life-changing, life-appreciating or life-aware. There are times, more than I'd like to admit, when I forget how precious life is; then I quickly remind myself that the precariousness of life is so near. I think of Hurricane Katrina. Or the earthquake in Haiti. The tsunami in Japan. In an instant it can all be but a memory.

Not luck

With grief, there is always getting through the poignant and significant songs, the memorable places, the comfort foods, and the smells that set off explosions or implosions in your heart. For many years, there was an unspoken, almost superstitious tradition of having a red front door and/or black and white tiles somewhere in the place that we lived. I'm not sure when or where it began, possibly with the apartment my parents shared in Holland. We had a red door and black and white tiles on West Brookline Street in Boston; we had only the tiles in the hallway of the apartment on Riverside Drive in NYC; we again had the red door and the tiles in the house on Robin Road in Englewood and finally at the house on Cedar Lane in Teaneck.

However, the door of the last house they decided would be replaced with a soft pale yellow. Perhaps if they'd stuck with the red door, it would have helped the karma of that house. From the moment they bought it, it fought them and they seemed to battle an endless series of negative spirals downward. This tradition of door and tiles continued with my own family until just recently. In fact, when we were looking for our first house, I walked through the front door to be greeted by the familiar black and white tiles

I'd grown up with. This was my first house shortly after my father died. I naturally took it as a sign. My father was most definitely there to welcome us home.

I don't believe in luck or happenstance. I do believe in a supreme being and in the spirits of our universe who are in a divine order to help guide us. I believe this is true if we are willing to remain open and in the frame of mind to receive it. Slowly, over the course of months and years, the tunes that could at one time destroy me began to fill me with gratefulness and uplifting memories. The places that stirred an eerie longing began wrapping me once again in comfort and a welcomed familiarity. The foods started to look more appetizing and taste delicious again. The sights, sounds, and the smells helped remind me of all I had been graced with, in all its many variations, over and over again.

Familiar things

My father taught me to take the time for listening, for hearing, for savoring, and for smelling the most beautiful and special things in life. It never ceases to stun me, the way a gentle waft of a certain something can so completely transport me, without transition, to another moment in time. In a blink, I am four years old again lying on my father's stomach in the shade on Paradise Island. In that moment, I hear the sea in the big white and pale pink conch shell I kept for years. I feel the hot sun on my shoulder blades and the weird but warmly familiar sand between my little toes. Perhaps it is through my father's recollections that I know the memory, but somehow it is so alive here within me. It asks only for the slightest jog of recollection or the sight of a conch shell to make it real all over again.

On a warm and sunny day, my father broke my heart for the final bittersweet time. It had been about a year after his death that I went into my closet to feel comfort. There was comfort and safety in the smell of a few things I'd kept that he'd worn. I had found those few things—a worn out black T-shirt with the words "Surrender Dorothy!" on it, one of several beautiful butter-leather jackets he coveted, a few scarves and pocket squares, and a couple of caps. I needed to smell a memory and nestle into something warm and familiar that reminded me of him. Of course, everything reminded me of him. I suppose I needed that instant flashback to occur—the one that makes you reel and swoon with the authenticity of it all. These are moments brought on

NOT SO BLACK AND WHITE

by a specific trigger. When that connection is made to that smell, that song, that place or certain shadow on the trees, it courses through you with a current of remembering so fierce, it leaves you staggering.

I wanted to make that connection; to relive a memory through a scent that *was* my father and that comforted me. And what was it and is it about his scent that draws me still? Within its rich and spicy fragrance lived so many of my memories with him: the good and the difficult. It's as if I should be able to open his green glass bottle of the scent and pour out those memories. They are fragrant associations of my life with my father. His fragrance and smell was just as colorful, as complicated, and as simple as he was. Like his life, his aroma was a collage of events, loves, and losses that made up the unique and interesting fabric of his existence.

What smelled of him I cherished and mourned. I mourned a devoted daughter's pain of losing her hero. Those sacred scents had remained and were left behind for my remembering; those invisible wafts of wonder that lingered when he'd gone. They hid in places throughout the house. They sat at his desk and permeated his sheets, his colorful scarves, and his beautiful clothes. Although they did seem at times to loom and descend over me powerfully, they never soured on my tongue or turned to vinegar in my nostrils. They always remained a lovely reminder of his strong person, his love of life and of us. In those smells I felt a lot closer to his childhood, his choices, his travels, his memories, and his essence. Those scents were years in collecting and they came together deliciously to create what so many of us have come to know as *Daddy's smell*.

Familiar things can be wonderful. The things that remind me of childhood, of first loves, of graduations and of opening nights, are the things that keep me connected: Our touch, a baby's delicate soft skin; our taste: dripping cold ice cream in a sugar cone on a hot August night and our smell: a cool dewy morning after a long spring rain. And for me it was also my father's scent.

So into my closet I went, one sunny afternoon alone in my house, to find one of his shirts or scarves because I needed that scent to feel safe. I missed him so much. So much that I went through my mornings swallowing air, through my days being reminded that he was indeed nowhere on this earth to be found, and through my nights filling up like a balloon with creeping anxiety and Rescue Remedy. I missed him so much that like a romantic junkie I searched for my fix. I pulled down a T-shirt and pushed it into my face. Nothing. No smell, no scent, no recognizable Cerutti or Vetiver or Eau Sauvage, no Dad.

My heart sank. I pulled down another and another! Nothing. I remember feeling angry and cheated, then sad as I exhaled onto the soft bed. I cried quietly. That rush of familiar abandonment engulfed me. And that loneliness! It was so confusing to me. How could those scents and smells, in an instant, vanish? I blamed him. How could he take them away from me, knowing how badly I needed them? For more than a year, they remained strong, with no hint of ever fading. I needed them to remain in the grain of wood, in the flower vase, in the big wing chair, trapped between the pictures and the frame, and in the very oil of my skin. However, he had clearly taken them unannounced one day or night when I was not paying attention.

Yet, as I surrendered the essence of him, there remained other reminders. Occasionally, I can still hear the easy abandon in his laughter. I see him in my daughters: in their small expressions of a crooked mouth or wry way about them. I see his gifts in my first child's dancing and choreography. I see him in my younger daughter's clear, honest look at the world and her fierce determination. I sometimes see him in their walk. When they walk ahead of me, sometimes it is *he*. He walks between them holding their small hands and smiles. He is truly in heaven as I experience this walking dream. The girls fade away and he moves out in front with his red silk shirt flying open in the breeze. He's confident with his comfortable gait; his feet turned out. He stops. His hand is on his hip while the other hand adjusts his expensive tortoise-shell sunglasses atop his small, round head. He asks me what I see in the store window. I look again in the window, turn to him, and he is gone. He is gone, vanished, drifted with the scents that left me as well. On another day I'll turn a corner and there he'll be; in the surprise of that familiar wonderfully rich and exciting scent that was my father, come to walk me safely home.

CHAPTER 14

A STRANGE LOVE

BEFORE HAVING CHILDREN of my own, I knew I needed to give voice to all that I'd kept bottled up inside of me since age ten or eleven. All those years of anger, hurt and disappointment had never been shared with a single soul. And so when my therapist asked me at thirty-one years old, "Where is your mother in all of this?" I thought I might die from the pain of it all. I did not die. I threw it all up over and over and over again, until I gradually nursed myself, with the unending rock support of my husband, back to psychological and emotional health. Naturally, I remain on the road to recovery; trying to change the patterns, forgive myself, forgive my mother, and live a loving life. These life lessons are life-long.

While watching the *Oprah* show one day, it occurred to that we seldom hear about the *mother* abandoning her children. Perhaps it doesn't happen as often as a father's departure, but it does happen, and I can assure you the consequences are devastating. I have a suspicion that because the concept is often inconceivable, we'd rather not bring it up. I am also quite certain the complexities concerning my mother and her choices are such that several lifetimes would not unearth my myriad questions. Nonetheless, I continued to ask the questions and privately hoped that continual conversation with her might change things or at least spark the memories I buried when I, figuratively speaking, laid her to rest so many years ago.

It was not until after my father's death that the smallest portal reopened. It has been within that tiny space that we have attempted at something. I came to the conclusion that assuming a parental role with my mother was the only hope I had if I wanted to maintain any conversation or connection between us. I learned to bite my tongue and not to confront her. The choice to exist with her on these terms was inspired by the birth of my children. It was my hope for them to have a connection with their only living grandmother. As fate would have it, I was blessed with two girls: clearly a second chance at getting the mother/daughter scenario absolutely perfect. Frankly and with the challenge of perfection aside, I wouldn't have it any other way.

In the early '90s, my mother returned to her birthplace of Arnhem, Holland to be, quite naturally, yet ironically, near her mother. She told us all years ago that her father had died, which at the time, we didn't know if we could believe. Since then, it seems her daily life is simple. She is alone and remains as elusive as always, never divulging what she does or how she spends her time. Our infrequent conversations remain always on the surface and stay placid.

Until recently, my mother and brother continued to be in touch almost daily. They have always shared a special bond and a mutual understanding of one another. In this way, it allows them to be who they are, no questions asked. However, the "don't ask, don't tell" policy is almost the polar opposite of how I function. There is somewhere in that an element of grace and acceptance that I simply do not possess. It is also a thing that I have somewhat admired. It has always been more difficult for me to surrender in life. In the recent past, it seemed I'd found my own way of keeping the line of communication open, with most of my sanity and strange love for her intact.

It is a peculiar love and so is my understanding of the woman who brought me into this world. She has been a distant dream of longing. She has floated on the outskirts of my wishing for something improbable. In the summer of 2006, I concluded that "something" to be impossible. After sixteen years of not laying eyes upon her—not since leaving her in the train station in Rotterdam—I agreed, along with my brother, to meet her for lunch in Manhattan.

I was there on business, but I heard from a friend that she was in town. I'd also learned from this friend that Parker had planned to *surprise* me by showing up with her at an artist fundraising event. Knowing that this would create certain shock and possible disaster, my friend contacted me to give me a heads-up. Needless to say, I was greatly appreciative and called my brother immediately.

The three of us did arrange to have lunch my first day in town, but I was resolved to keep it brief and on my terms as much as possible. I was okay until I got into the cab that took me from Tribeca to the Upper West Side. While in the cab, I suffered a sudden panic attack. My stomach turned itself into a painful knot and I was somewhat terrified. I thought to myself, *What am I doing? Why did I agree to do this?* I spoke to Byron on the phone while I was in the cab. He asked with trepidation, "Are you excited to see her?" I replied flatly, "No, I'm not excited to see her."

I wanted to jump ship, but I was almost there, and my brother was really counting on me to make an attempt at some kind of peace offering. The first "tell" of our meeting was that she didn't recognize me when I bent down to say hello, peering into Parker's little sports car with her in the passenger seat. Maybe I misunderstood her reaction. It's difficult to imagine her not remembering her own daughter, so we'll leave that one up for grabs. However, I did glean two monumental truths from our lunch together. The first being that I finally came to adequately articulate how I feel—how I've often felt—in relationship to my mother. I felt that I was sitting with my *brother's* mother because there has always existed that lack of mother/daughter connection between us. I looked at my brother continuously and he was positively high that we were all there together. I was happy and sad for him. The second discovery later threw me into a spin of being literally sick for three days when I returned home.

We were all sitting together in the tiny Italian restaurant on Columbus Avenue being very pleasant—and me unable to eat a bite—when I asked, "So, Mom, when are you going to see my girls?" The sidebar is that she was in the States staying with my brother and had planned to stay a month or more before going back to Holland.

At this point, I'm holding my breath because I'm worried she'll want to stay with *me* for a month. I couldn't have been more wrong. She replied, "Well … I don't know Holly. I have to go to Boston and L.A. and …" For me, lunch was over. Nowhere in that reply was even the vaguest consideration of making a way to see her grandchildren. I was in shock, as was Parker. He knew how much that blow hurt me. I felt, yet again, completely unprepared and sideswiped by this ultimate disappointment.

The full impact of her words was waiting for me at the threshold of my house when I returned to the safety of my family. I disintegrated into a pool of depression that took a couple months to come out of fully. The depression did not last and the emotional reeling settled. Yet and still, if only for my children, I have remained determined to find a way to make it all make sense. Or maybe not. Everyone hopes for a fairy tale ending, but often in real time, in real life, we don't get that wish. Life is much more complicated, unpredictable, and messy.

Although I am now a grown woman with a family of my own, in a still quiet and private place, I continue to wish for the improbable. That little girl is still inside of me believing in the fairy dust. The grown-up in me knows better and keeps shouting, "Snap out of it!" How to bridge the gap, live within the balance, not end up angry or bitter?

We both still wander this planet. She is desperately afraid to face the reality of the choices she made yet she is here & never to recover yet I am here. My father, her husband, has died. She and I, with all of our imperfections and pain, are alive. What will we do with it all? We are all in some ways tough and in more ways so fragile. I do believe the cliché *what doesn't kill you makes you stronger* and hopefully wiser. Love must prevail. Though that love may have to seep sneakily in from afar, for my own emotional self-preservation and for my children's, I must believe it is still possible.

A month following the lunch with my mother and Parker, he was arrested. Right before that happened, my mother had extended her month-long stay with him for a week more. Almost immediately following his arrest, she was on the plane back to Europe. I thought to myself, *And this is supposed to be her favored child.* She commented to Parker's wife, "God will take care of it," and she was on a plane. I was completely astonished, though I probably shouldn't have been, and deeply sad for my brother. And although God may ultimately have the last word on what will become of Parker or any of us, the only thing I could think was *how sad*. How sad that she'd missed yet another opportunity to make up for the mother she hadn't been. The only response to her story must be love. I must find it within me to be this way. I *must* find it within me to be this way.

Chapter 15

MY GLORIOUS FAMILY

What doesn't kill you makes you stronger. This was one of the overused sentiments, about things challenging, that we Wilsons lived by. The philosophy was to feel the pain, honor it. and move on, with emphasis on "move on" because *life's too short* and, of course, *it's not over 'til the fat lady sings.* This tough look at challenges is a way of life that has become a part of my skin; a part of who I am, and at times it has served me well. It is a philosophy that helps to keep me from giving up and lifts me out of my muck and mire to carry on. Despite this very black and white approach to things, which sometimes seem insurmountable, I have come to realize that life is not so black and white but much more colorful.

With each monumental event, as the years rolled on, I began to take quiet stock of things with a nagging need to search for deeper understanding. The onset of Chip's challenges provoked a questioning within me that demanded more truth about all things, which began with myself. Little by little, during those difficult times, I began to unlock my Pandora's Box and within the box were many other boxes, each with its own unique and mystifying gift. Some were blood-soaked, as I thought about the anger and disappointment I had concerning my mother, while other boxes were magical, exciting, and positively divine as I recalled the life of showbiz that kept us bubbling with energy and inspiration. Each of us possesses our own Pandora's Box of experiences and emotions. We embrace them, curse them, or demand an explanation, based on who we are and what we need.

I think back on the morning I walked in on my mother's private moment. An array of new feelings and judgments were born for me on that day. For many years there was a small place within me that shuddered when in the presence of an interracial couple. It conjured up my mother and father's union gone badly—the obvious template for every interracial couple's inevitable failure.

I didn't go through the more expected struggle with my identity: am I black or white? I always identified with being African American, even during periods when most of my friends were not. At the same time, I also didn't deny being half white. I struggled more with the topic of the interracial relationship. My younger experience misguidedly suggested that the differences between people were too great and the price too high to believe that love could last. However, when I was able to move below my surface to the place deep inside of me where all is possible and my dreams are infinite, the truth told me otherwise. It brings to mind what the writer James Baldwin once said, "Love is like the lightening bolt. Love is where you find it." This point of view is something I was born with; I came into the world because of it and grew up being engulfed by it. Somewhere along the way, I'd forgotten this was my core belief.

I eventually grew into remembering that love is often bigger than our idea of what it's *supposed* to be. My parents knew this. They trusted love and took it on. I am so proud of their choice. And I am equally proud of my father and Chip's choice. For as complicated, non-traditional—or even to some seemingly *unnatural*—as it was sometimes perceived, their fearless love for one another was never anything less than a lifelong devoted commitment. Parker, Chip, my father, and I, individually or as a family, at times questioned the resilience it took to choose the family we had created for ourselves. We, each in our own time, accepted the challenge because despite all that may have not been perfect, we had much laughter and much love among us. Therein lay our success—our success as a family—even with all of our private chaos.

I have come to embrace the fact that anything worth loving is worth fighting like hell to keep. Today I know that all my differences have only worked to my ultimate advantage. And I conclude that the more I am able to love the union that produced me and the uniqueness of the family who raised, encouraged and supported me, the more likely I am to love all of who I am that much more.

My father was fearless. At the same time, he had doubts and insecurities like everyone else, but he wasn't a prisoner to them. His greater hunger for being better and using his gifts spurred him on. He was fearless in his choice to dance at a time when little black boys weren't doing that, in making a grand life for himself for more than ten years in a foreign land, in choosing to love across the color line and producing biracial children in a racist world. He was fearless in returning to his country in the heat of revolution as he accepted invitations to head dance and theatre departments at some of the most prestigious universities, armed with the conviction that he could make them thrive. With each new opportunity, he rose to the challenge and succeeded. He did this as he entered the world of Broadway and took it consistently by storm and when he chose custody of his two young children and again when he chose Chip—the man who would share his life for eighteen years, until their deaths. He was beautifully fearless to the very end.

From him I learned, saw, and felt the painful glory of watching a sunset. He remains beside me or above me now, sharing in my exploration and whispering, "Look at those colors! Do you see that orange?" And of course I do. Now I share these tender gifts with my own children. The importance of taking the time to breathe in God's gifts to us is essential to our gratefulness of all things. This priceless pleasure has made me feel soft and kept me strong. Not only did he have a wonderful sense of style, but he was also willing and pleased to be humbled by life's everyday miracles. These daily, hourly experiences inspired him. He drew from it, as great artists do. He shared with me the gift of loving nature and relishing the sumptuousness of the tiniest happenings, in a big, overwhelming, and often gross world.

He taught my brother and me the brilliance of color, the mystery of flowers, and the grace and power of wildlife. These things I never learned at school. I soaked up his insights and sensitivities. He was always teaching and exploring. It was through his inexhaustible appetite to rediscover and evolve that I was touched and so many were also affected. Geoffrey Holder expressed it at my father's memorial when he said, "Billy was always a child. Always seeing things for the first time." Many people have let a thousand sunsets pass them by. I don't want to be one of those people. So when I ache, as myriad colors unfurl with the sun rising or when I cry every time I hear Mahler's *Fifth*, it is because of him that I am moved in this way.

This is the man who was my example. I now regard the greatness of his example as I make way for my own. I attempt to live in the moment of gratitude for the love in my life and for the sparkle in the long-lashed beauty of my daughters' clear eyes. Now I take digital snapshots of my daughters on *their* father's chest. I realize how lucky I am to have a beautiful man by my side to inspire my desire to live my life more fully, more fearlessly, and more happily than ever. Byron and our two beautiful girls are a few of the biggest examples of what I've done right in my life as I have moved forward.

My desire is to have loved and to depart with love around me. It is how, I hope, my father felt when he left us. There were many moments that allowed him time to reflect on his loves, his losses, and his successes. He told me hilarious stories about things I never knew existed, he confessed mistakes he'd made and all of the many things he'd hoped to do. He always wanted to go to Brazil, he wanted to choreograph for film, he thought maybe he'd treat himself to a Jaguar, he wanted to see my children. Whether a sad or funny conversation between us, he always, almost without exception, remained grateful for all the many blessings: the work he was able to produce and the people he'd known and loved. He held an awesome respect for the bigger picture of what life had to offer. He never lost his sense of humor or his humility. So while death and our beloved losses may be cruel, the spirit leaves behind pieces of dreams that lived and breathed hard while they were here.

This journey is miraculous, mysterious, comical, and at times incredibly fragile. To me, it is all to be embraced. I welcome it knowing that at the end of having survived another bit of it, I am adding more to a legacy of strength, compassion—and, I pray, wisdom. I like to think that some of my father's wisdom has rubbed off on me. It is not enough only to recite wisdom. It is essential to live it. I have always spent more time in my "head" than in my body, despite the fact that I was a dancer. Living life is not spent in one's mind. For most of us anyway, we attempt to live with every part of who we are. It has been one of my goals to live presently and to enjoy each new discovery within its process. Most days I fall short, but I keep trying, determined that one day I will truly get it. In the in-between time, at the heart of living day to day, I want to enjoy this ride. I want to love hard and exist with more humor, and to spin feeling as much as I can without as much fear as possible. What I do know for certain is that being in my father's care, not only as a dancer, but also as his daughter, was safe. Feeling safe gives you wings even when flying seems like the most terrifying thing in the world.

∽ᴓᴖ

Epilogue

THIS WONDERFUL LIFE

A S MY HEAD turns to the right, I'm reminded of being in flight and how much at home I feel. I had a father who soared. And although all grown up now, I am still his little girl trying desperately to make him proud of my flight. I realize it is time now for me to plunge fearlessly. As I did when I stood fiercely concentrated at the ballet barre, as I did when rejected by my mother and when I was faced with the pages of *Velvet Magazine*. As I did when I pushed through the nerves of auditions—often doubting that I was good enough. As I did when I was ashamed of my family and fighting the fear of never finding a good man to love me and all of my luggage. As I did when faced with news of AIDS, fighting AIDS, losing the battle to AIDS, and losing Chip and my father in the same year.

It is my responsibility to use the wings I was born with to fly, but ultimately to soar! Although I don't feel my father's physical hand supporting my lower back, his spirit is more powerful than ever.

As we make our final descent to land at Schiphol Airport in Amsterdam, I am thinking it must be possible to have it all, whatever that means to you. For me, it means having the wealth of my children around me, having the marriage deepen, great friends, laughing more, great escapes, sounds, sights, tastes, healing the wounds with my mother—if only on my own—and hoping that wherever "Billy" sits or perhaps dances, he looks down on me and can say: "What a wonderful life you are creating, Holly. I'm so proud of you!" The only mirror I still hold up is one of living my life fearlessly, as he did. The only thing I know is that he would have wanted me to do it my way.

"There's an old woman working in a garden some yards away. She is wearing a housedress and white rubber boots. There are red and rather pinkish chickens feeding in that small field. There are still clouds and the sky is a grey and silver wash but underneath it all is a kind of luminous glow, rather like a promise of something better. But then nature is always perfection, whether benign or violent. Our task is to live close enough with her to learn some of her secrets and enrich our imperfect lives."

(Taken from Billy Wilson's diary
September 9, 1972: Forte dei Marmi, Italy)

ACKNOWLEDGMENTS

THERE IS NO way I could have gotten this far without the tireless loving support and encouragement from the individuals I am about to mention.

I first want to acknowledge my mother, my father, Chip, and my brother for creating the uniquely complicated and incredibly rich family that provided all the fodder, the blood work, and the inspiration for my story.

Thank you, girlfriends—Allegra di Carpegna, Gabri Christa, Cynthia Garcia, Edith Hagigi, Leiani Ayala Seibert, Tasi Rigsby and Christina Johnson, for helping to keep me sane. Your female wisdom, honesty, and strength have been my emotional lifeboat many times and many years over. Each of you holds a divine space in my heart.

Thank you, Mr. Maurice Hines, Todd Hunter, Michael McElroy and Phyllis Kauffman Sager, for all your sage advice and for keeping me laughing!

Thank you Jean Wu and I Cheng Huang of Zen Cha, for being my writing home away from home. Many thanks to Brian Caiazza and his staff of TRUE Studios for working so hard on my site, being patient with my overwhelmed brain, and creating a most interesting and provocative cover for my book.

ACKNOWLEDGMENTS

Thank you, David Campbell, for the first offering of spot-on edits, and Gretchen Hirsch, for your professional corrections, tasteful choices, and genuine words of encouragement.

Thank you, Lisa Leguillou, for entering my world when you have. I can't wait to make stage magic with you!

Thank you, Mayor Michael B. Coleman, for your sincere interest and belief in the importance of my story and reminding me to "walk through the door."

Thank you, Kasi Lemmons, my friend. You have been my stellar example of a woman and an artist who has been *doing* and doing it with depth, intelligence and beauty. Thank you for swallowing my book whole, when you had zero time in La La Land, and then telling me, "This is also a movie, Holly, and Vondie and I want to do it." We've still got work to do. Love you, Kas.

Thank you, Anthony Barrile. "Hi, honey." You have been my friend, partner in NYC movie marathons since we were fifteen, and one of my most important creative compasses throughout this book's evolution. Thank you for your friendship, your brilliant mind, and the witty quips that helped talk me down off the ledge and kept me in stitches while in "the waiting room." You also happen to be one of Broadway's great hidden treasures. Your knowledge, impeccable producer's intuition, and enormous generosity are just a few of your priceless qualities. And eternal thanks for my book's perfect, perfect title!

Thank you, Blair Underwood, my old and cherished friend. You have remained in my corner all these years, encouraging, challenging, and persistently doing all you can to help get my story out there. We've met with agents, editors, turned ideas over and upside-down trying to find the magical key leading to the perfect combination. Of course, the magic is just the process, and the work is the only thing. Your largesse has exceeded expectation and I gratefully "receive." And a special thank you for opening your heart by providing this book with a lovely foreword.

Byron, my other half, my soul mate, husband, and exquisite father of our children, you have been my most patient angel. Thank you for ushering me out of the house to Starbuck's at 6 a.m. to write when our firstborn was only weeks old. You and our two beauties are the reasons I have persevered. Thank you for putting up with all of Mom's crankiness and for understanding that parents have goals and dreams also. You guys are my greatest joy and evidence of all the love I received from my father and Chip gone right. To my three unconditionally loving cheerleaders, I love you more than Daddy's pasta!

A NOTE OF THANKS...

A special collective thank you to all those photographers who are responsible for the beautiful images in my book. I feel incredibly fortunate to have had these cherished photos to share with all of you. The photographers who have not been acknowledged, have not been forgotten. It has been my sincerest intention to include all photo credits as much as possible. If any of my readers can share information regarding photo credit, I welcome it and will happily include them in future reprints of this book.

On behalf of my father and me, a heart felt thanks to all the photographers for your artistry and taste.

Most sincerely,
Alexis Wilson

Made in the USA
Lexington, KY
05 July 2012